MAKING
YouTube®
VIDEOS

WILEY

MAKING

YouTube®

VIDEOS

2nd Edition

by Nick Willoughby, with
Tee Morris and Will Eagle

WILEY

Making YouTube® Videos, 2nd Edition

Published by: **John Wiley & Sons, Inc.**, 111 River Street, Hoboken, NJ 07030-5774, www.wiley.com

Copyright © 2020 by John Wiley & Sons, Inc., Hoboken, New Jersey

Published simultaneously in Canada

Contents

Project 3: Edit   73

Project 4: Creating a Gameplay Video · 115

Project 5: Share · 144

INTRODUCTION

HELLO FUTURE YOUTUBERS! Welcome to *Making YouTube Videos*, 2nd Edition — the book that does exactly what it says on the cover.

You want to be the next YouTube star? Do you find yourself watching YouTube videos and thinking, "I could do that!" or "I really want to do that"? Well, you've picked up the right book.

Millions of people are uploading their videos to YouTube — and there's plenty of room for you, too. All you need is to turn the creative ideas in your head into videos. You're going to have so much fun, and we're going to guide you through every step.

ABOUT YOUTUBE

YouTube started in 2005 for people all over the world to share videos. We can't imagine that anyone could have guessed how successful it would become. Would you have guessed it?

And now, if you want to learn how to do something, watch gameplay, or laugh at funny videos, where do you go? YouTube. And did you know that some people make YouTube videos as their job? How fun would that be?

WARNING

Your safety is the most important thing. Don't include any personal information in the videos you share on YouTube. Don't tell anyone online what your name is or where you live.

ABOUT THIS BOOK

They don't teach you how to make YouTube videos at school, do they? If they do, you go to an awesome school.

INTRODUCTION

In *Making YouTube Videos*, we share what we've learned to help you make films. (We wish we had this book when we were kids. That would be impossible, of course, unless we'd had a time machine for us and for YouTube.)

They say that a wise person learns from his mistakes and a clever person learns from other people's mistakes. We've learned everything we know from working in different areas within the filmmaking industry, and the mistakes we made along the way made us better. The great thing is that you get to avoid making a bunch of the mistakes that we made. You may still make mistakes, but it's important to never give up!

In this book, you

» Explore the different cameras you can use

» Discover how to record sound

» Find out how to light your scenes

» Edit your video

» Capture and edit gameplay from a console or computer

» See ways to share your videos on YouTube

» Discover how to get more views and subscribers on YouTube

Sometimes, you'll see a URL (web address) for forms or examples we've placed online for you. You can find those extras at www.dummies.com/go/making youtubevideos2e.

Some figures will have a magnifying glass, like you see here. The glass is drawing attention to the parts of the screen you use. The highlighted text draws your attention to the figure.

ABOUT YOU

You're interested in making movies. That's why you're here reading this, right?

We also figure that you have a way to capture film (a camera or phone) and a way to edit it (a computer or laptop).

We would bet that you've been online before and know all about clicking icons, and that you've pressed the Record button on a camera.

ABOUT THE ICONS

As you read the projects in this book, you'll see a few icons. The icons point out different things:

WARNING

If something might be dangerous, or if it's something you shouldn't choose, you see this Warning icon.

REMEMBER

The Remember icon tells you the most important ideas. This is information you'll use all the time when making films.

TIP

We use the Tip icon whenever we have information or advice that might help you with your film project.

DID YOU KNOW THERE ARE BILLIONS OF VIDEOS ON YOUTUBE? Billions! And that people add 300 hours of video every minute? That's a lot of videos.

YouTube is a great way to share with your friends and family the videos you make. Don't worry if you haven't made a video yet. We're going to help you make your very own YouTube video as you read this book.

FOLLOW THE VIDEO-MAKING PROCESS

You can divide the video-making process into these five main stages:

- » Development
- » Preproduction
- » Production
- » Post-production
- » Distribution

If you imagine the video-making process as a trip, these five main stages are stops on the way. You can't get where you're going unless you go to each place along the way.

DEVELOPMENT

Development is one of the most important areas of the process — and it can be one of the hardest. It's usually the longest part of video-making because it's important to get the concept and the story right before moving into preproduction.

The development stage means completing these tasks:

- » Coming up with ideas and themes to create a story that has a good beginning, middle, and end

- » Building the story so that it's ready to take into preproduction; that is, writing a script for the actors to work from and, sometimes, a storyboard for the director and crew to work from

A *storyboard* is a series of images that help you plan which shots to film.

PREPRODUCTION

The preproduction stage uses the idea, story, script, and storyboard to prepare for the production stage. In preproduction, everything is planned as much as possible.

WARNING

If you rush or skip preproduction, something may go wrong and it could take you longer to film.

Preproduction takes place when you

» Choose actors.

» Find locations.

» Build sets for each scene.

» Plan each filming day.

» Organize rehearsals for the actors.

The work you do on these steps saves you time in the production and post-production stages.

PRODUCTION

The *production* stage is where the story and characters come to life as you film.

In the production stage, you

» Run rehearsals for the actors to learn their lines and to develop their characters.

» Set up camera equipment on location.

» Film the scenes you planned.

» Review the filmed footage to make sure you've captured everything and that it looks good enough to edit.

POST-PRODUCTION

The *post-production* stage is when you piece together the footage you captured during production. This stage is exciting. You get to see the results of all the hard work you put into the previous stages and also get to watch the video come together in the *editing tool* — that piece of software where video clips are imported, arranged into one video, and then exported for your audience to watch.

Post-production includes

» Importing the footage on a computer

» Editing in software like iMovie, Filmora, or HitFilm

» Adding music or sound effects or other kinds of enhancements

DISTRIBUTION

Distribution is the final stage in the journey to make a video. At this point, your film has been produced and edited. Now it's ready for the audience to enjoy.

This can be a worrisome time for you because the audience will make comments and give reviews.

Most blockbuster films are first distributed to theaters and then released on DVD, but you'll distribute your video by YouTube.

GATHER YOUR TOOLS

A professional filmmaker could spend a fortune on tools. However, to get started, you need only a few basic tools, and most of them aren't expensive:

» **Video camera:** Without a video camera, there is no video. A video camera captures the picture and audio and stores them on a media card, hard drive, flash drive, or tape.

REMEMBER

A video camera can take different forms, which you can read more about in the next section.

» **Microphone:** The microphone captures sound, which can be recorded with the video to a media card, hard drive, flash drive, or tape. The microphone can be built into your camera or not. (And in that case, it's *external.*) Project 2 teaches you more about using a microphone for audio.

» **Light source:** Your audience needs to see your subjects, so light is quite important. The source can be a natural one (like the sun) or an artificial one (like a lamp). Project 2 helps you with lighting.

» **Editing tool:** An *editing tool* is a computer program where you import video footage, slice it up, and arrange it, ready for your audience to view. Project 3 is all about editing.

» **Tripod:** A tripod is a great tool for keeping the camera steady in a *fixed* (single) position. It can be used to smoothly film moving subjects from left to right or up and down. Don't worry if you don't have a tripod — there are many inventive ways to keep your camera steady.

» **Media card/tape/flash drive/hard drive:** This device is where your camera stores video footage.

» **Headphones:** You can plug this device into a video camera or an external sound recorder to monitor the *quality* of the audio. How good is it?

HOW YOUR CAMERA WORKS

Don't worry: We're not going to bore you with details here — but it is useful to know the basics.

A video camera works a lot like your eye. Your eyes see things as a series of still images, or *frames.* Your brain then puts them together so fast that it looks like smooth movement — it's clever stuff, isn't it? The camera does a similar thing: It captures movement in a series of frames, or *still* images.

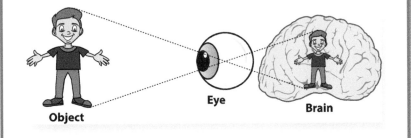

Object   **Eye**   **Brain**

(continued)

(continued)

Also like your eye, the camera records the images using light from the scene. The light enters the lens, and the images go on a microchip inside the digital video camera. These images go to your media card or tape.

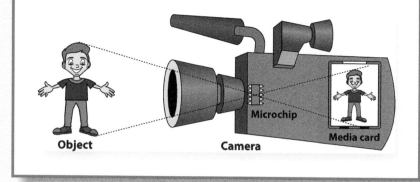

Object   Microchip   Media card

Camera

CHOOSE YOUR CAMERA

A digital video camera makes filmmaking easier and less expensive. It comes in different sizes, qualities, and prices. For under $100, you can buy a compact HD camcorder that records great video. Because you're starting out, this is completely reasonable.

High-definition (HD) cameras have better-quality images than the old *standard* definition (SD). HD cameras capture a larger image than SD with more vibrant colors and more detail. These images are measured in pixels. High Definition video has at least 1280 pixels wide by 720 pixels tall. Full HD video has 1920 pixels by 1080 pixels. You may have seen this information when buying a TV.

CHECK YOUR TEMPERATURE

This may sound odd, but light comes in different colors. A candle has a warm orange look. A clear blue sky has a colder blue look. The color of light is measured in a unit called *Kelvin*. You can adjust this setting on your camera using the white balance controls, or by simply setting your camera to auto white balance. This setting adjusts the color temperature for you to match the light in your scene.

4K and Ultra-High Definition video is taking over with more video cameras and camera phones recording video twice as wide and twice as high as full HD, which is 3840 pixels by 2160 pixels. That's a lot of pixels!

At the other extreme, you can find video cameras that cost over $50,000. Professionals use those cameras to shoot blockbuster movies — but even those cameras have downsides.

As a filmmaker, I like to use different types of digital video cameras for different reasons. The following sections describe the different types of digital video cameras.

BACK IN THE OLD DAYS

Traditional film cameras captured footage as a bunch of still images. The images were on light-sensitive tape running through the camera. This reel of tape was expensive to buy, and you couldn't reuse it. It also made it tough to set up and check shots.

Traditional film cameras create what we call a *cinematic* look, which makes the image look softer than you can with digital video. With traditional cameras you can, for example, blur backgrounds and make your subject stand out. It's harder to get this cinematic look with a digital video camera, especially with less expensive camcorders, which often have trouble with the lighter and darker areas of a shot, and whose images tend to be sharper.

WEBCAMS

A *webcam* plugs directly into your computer. It's affordable, easy to set up, and great for recording someone talking to the computer (like you might do when filming vlogs, reviews, or instructional videos, for example). Most desktop computers and laptops come with webcams.

If you want to film your YouTube video using a webcam but your computer doesn't have one built in, look online or in stores. They start around $20.

I use a webcam to record video blogs because it's simple to set up. A webcam makes it easy to edit and upload in a shorter amount of time.

CAMERA PHONES

A *camera phone* is a cell phone that captures still and moving images. Camera phones are smaller and lighter than most cameras, which makes it easier to capture video in smaller spaces. Camera phone manufacturers are constantly improving the features and quality of their devices, including the ability to record 4K footage and better image stabilization. Some feature films are now being shot using camera phones.

Camera phones don't usually offer the best quality for picture or sound, but they're great for capturing video simply and quickly.

TIP

Because camera phones are perfect for capturing random moments that are harder to capture with larger cameras, I use them to capture video and pictures for behind-the-scenes projects.

SOMETIMES ONE IS BETTER THAN TWO

For years, cameras used two lenses — one through which the photo was captured on film and another that passed the image to the *viewfinder* (which is what the photographer looks through). This approach had some problems: Sometimes photographers didn't get the pictures they thought they were getting. The single-lens reflex camera (and later, the digital single-lens reflex camera, or DSLR) changed that: With the single lens, the image you see in the viewfinder is the same as the one you see in pictures.

CAMCORDERS

A *camcorder* is a handheld video camera designed to record video and audio. Unlike DSLRs and digital cinema cameras (see the later section "DSLR and mirrorless video"), camcorders usually have lenses built in, which makes setting up and filming quicker and easier. Over the years, camcorders have become less expensive, and they offer better video and sound quality than ever.

You can choose from many types of camcorders, starting with basic (around $100) all the way up to broadcast cameras (over $50,000).

You can put camcorders in two groups: affordable and professional. I think affordable is the way to go!

AFFORDABLE CAMCORDERS

The affordable range of camcorders offers some great features and fantastic quality. Most of the cameras in this group offer automatic functions, like these:

- » **Autofocus:** Focuses on the subject instead of on the background
- » **Face detection:** Focuses on the people in the shot
- » **Auto iris:** Adjusts brightness, depending on the light
- » **Auto white balance:** Adjusts the color temperature of the video image

Camcorders in this range are small, light, and easy to work with. They're great for shooting home videos.

PROFESSIONAL CAMCORDERS

I suppose I could have called this section "Unaffordable camcorders." Professional filmmakers need more from their cameras than most mere mortals do. Professionals sometimes need to take manual control and bypass the camcorder's brain altogether. We all know people are smarter than computers.

Who uses these fancy things? Teams recording outside news as well as production companies for the movies you see at the local theater.

Usually, the higher you go in the range of professional camcorders, the bigger the cameras get and the more manual features they have. The bigger camcorders are heavy! Twenty pounds may not sound like a lot, but it gets tough carrying that much weight around and trying to hold it steady for long.

ACTION CAMERAS

Camera makers are fitting more stuff into less space. This leads to the *action camera,* a small (half the size of a pack of playing cards), light camcorder that you can strap to yourself or to your sports equipment, bike, or car — or even your dog.

With an action camera, you can record video that's usually hard to get. For example, a cyclist can attach an action camera to her helmet to record what she sees as she's cycling. Action cameras can also be attached to free runners, skiers, skydivers, and race car drivers. The footage from action cameras helps the audience feel involved.

Action cameras are a great, inexpensive way to capture high-quality video. You can pay as little as $50 for one.

TIP

An action camera doesn't always record the best sound. These cameras are for shots where you don't need or care much about audio.

AERIAL CAMERAS

Shots filmed from the sky can look amazing, and they're being used more often in film and TV. You can get aerial video by attaching cameras to drones or quadcopters and get stunning footage that you can't see from the ground.

Before drones and quadcopters were around, the only way to get footage from the sky was to shoot from a camera in a full-size helicopter. That isn't cheap. Aerial cameras give the same effect for a lot less money.

Lots of drones and quadcopters are for sale at camera stores, and most start around $50.

WARNING

In some places, you need a license to fly a drone or quadcopter. Make sure you know what the rules are where you live.

DSLR AND MIRRORLESS VIDEO

Basically, a *DSLR camera* is one that uses a mirror behind the lens to reflect what's happening through the lens into the eyepiece. A *mirrorless* camera is similar to a DSLR but without the mirror; it replaces the optical viewfinder with a digital viewfinder or screen. The DSLR and mirrorless cameras are still-photography cameras that use detachable lenses and produce some amazing images. Within the past ten years or so, the makers began including a video function with their DSLR cameras that allows you to capture beautiful video, too.

TIP

DSLR and mirrorless cameras are more compact than some digital cinema cameras, so they're great if you're traveling or shooting in small spaces.

DSLR video can look downright *cinematic*, which means it looks more like the quality you'd see in a blockbuster film at the theater.

» DSLR and mirrorless cameras have bigger sensors, which capture more of the scene — more light and a greater depth of field. *Depth of field* is the area of your shot that's in focus. A large depth of field has more of your shot in focus; a shallow depth of field has less of your shot in focus (so the area behind and in front of your subject may look blurry).

» Most DSLR and mirrorless cameras allow different lenses so that you can get a variety of shots. The different shots are explained in more detail in Project 2.

WARNING

DSLR and mirrorless cameras usually aren't great for recording long video clips. They can overheat, so they have a limited recording time.

Recording sound isn't easy, either. The built-in microphone is so-so at best. The camera makes quite a bit of noise while you're recording; the only way to connect an external microphone is to use a mini jack.

I used DSLR cameras for video when they were first released, and I've shot many short films using them. The video was great, but because of the DSLR's limits with sound, I recorded sound using a separate device and then matched the sound to the video later, during the editing process. If you're working on a large project, matching sound like this can take a long time.

DIGITAL CINEMA CAMERAS

A *digital cinema camera* is used to film larger projects, and it gives a more cinematic look. Like the camcorder, the digital cinema camera has become more affordable and smaller. Fifty years ago, you would've needed a truck to carry around your cinema camera and equipment, but now it can fit into your backpack.

You can buy a digital cinema camera from most large camera stores, and the cameras range from $1,000 to more than $60,000. Yeah. That isn't a misprint. That's more than a lot of cars cost.

Even though a digital cinema camera can fit into your backpack, it's usually bigger than most cameras. It's also usually the more expensive option: You buy the body of the camera and then buy attachments, including lenses and video monitors. Some of these attachments cost as much as the camera body.

A cinema camera tends to have more manual settings and can be complicated to set up. Because of this, I mainly use my cinema camera for dramas and projects I do for businesses.

BEFORE YOU PRESS THE RECORD BUTTON, GET PREPARED. Good preparation makes the other steps much easier. You prepare by choosing a style, creating an idea, and planning the shots.

Are you ready?

CHOOSE A STYLE

An idea. A theme.

What do you want to make a video about? What do you want it to do? Coming up with an idea can be one of the hardest parts of making videos, but it can be the most exciting, too.

Now is the time to decide on the type, or style. You can make one of these popular types:

» **How-to, or tutorial:** If you have a skill you want to show, you can create a how-to, or *tutorial,* video. It might show people how to play a song on the guitar or make an origami swan or put on make-up. Not much is off limits here.

» **Gaming, or let's play:** If you're a gamer and you want to show other people how good (or bad) you are at playing, you can create a let's-play video. Maybe you have some tips you want to share?

TIP

To create a gaming, or let's-play, video, you need to be able to record and capture the game footage and send it into an editing tool. We show you how to do that in the Project 4 chapter, later in this book.

» **Review:** Here's a great way to tell your YouTube audience what you think or how you feel. You can review a camera you bought or a film you watched or a place you visited — even a recipe you tried! You can also include photos and video clips of the product you're reviewing.

» **Funny:** You have probably seen loads of funny animal videos on YouTube, especially starring cats — cats in boxes, cats taking selfies, cats taking naps, and many, many more cats. People often record these videos with camera phones and, usually, they're events that can't be repeated. Does your pet do something funny?

» **Short films:** If you want to create a video that has a story to it, and you want to work with actors and create scripts, making a short film is for you. Your film can be *fictional* (made up) or *nonfictional* (true). For short films, you might want to use a camcorder.

ASK PERMISSION FIRST

Getting permission to film people is vitally important. You don't want someone you've filmed to change their mind and demand to be taken out — especially after you've finished editing and uploading the film to YouTube. To avoid this problem, ask the people in your film to complete a *model release form.* By signing the form, a person agrees that you can use their image in your film. After someone signs the release, they give up the right to change their minds later. We use a standard model release form. You can get a blank version by searching for the term *model release* at http://www.dummies.com/go/makingyoutubevideos2e.

» **Video blogs:** If you want to talk to your audience about an interesting topic or if you have an opinion about something, you can create a video blog (also known as a vlog). *Vlogs* are video diaries, usually filmed with webcams or smaller video recording devices.

How you can make your video stand out? How will your video be different?

THINK OF AN IDEA

How do you come up with a fresh idea for a video? That's hard to say. Sometime we've spent days, weeks, and even months thinking of ideas for films, but then we've also just been driving in a car or trying to get to sleep when an idea has popped into our heads.

When you've decided on a style, decide what your video is *about.*

Think about these questions when you're coming up with an idea:

» **What does your audience want**? Who *is* your audience? What do they want? Don't think only about what *you* want to do or what *you* think will work. Ask your audience — people you know who watch your sort of video. What would they like to see? Someone may give you the seed of an idea that you could help grow into something amazing.

» **What stories are out there**? Many films and videos are based on true stories. Do you, or does someone you know, have a story worth telling? Ask around. See what you can find. Most of the films we've written are based on events that have happened to us or to people we know. If you can't find a story from people you know, look through a few short-story books; they may inspire you.

» **What's possible?** Telling stories about aliens, monsters, and faraway planets can be good if you own a spaceship — but what kinds of stories can you film with the locations and props you already have? For inspiration, have a look around and see what's available to you.

Also, think about who can help make your video: Who will act? Who will hold the boom? It's okay to ask someone to help you write or brainstorm ideas. We've written a lot of films with a writing partner, which is great: One of us may come up with an idea, and the other person will throw in more ideas, and the story builds from there.

» **Is there a bad idea?** No. There's no such thing. Write down every idea you have. Any idea could become something great. You may write down loads of ideas you won't use for a while, but it never hurts to have more than you need. Any idea that's useless for your current project could well inspire your next story.

STRUCTURE YOUR VIDEO

When planning your YouTube video, it might be helpful to create a *structure*, which is defined this way:

REMEMBER

Every good story in every good video should have a good beginning, middle, and end. This applies to all video styles, including vlogs and tutorials.

Think about the following ingredients when you're structuring your video:

» **Introduction:** This is an important part of your video — it's when your audience decides to continue watching (or to bail out and do something else instead). The introduction should *captivate* your audience — grab their attention — and make them want to watch. It should introduce your topic or theme and your characters.

» **Ending:** This is where you leave your audience, which is also really important. By the end of the video, your audience will form opinions. You want people who watch to turn to the next person and say, "That was good!" or "That was funny." To get that reaction, make sure you've given what you promised in the title or introduction. Did your audience learn anything? Did they laugh? Were they entertained? The ending can include a thank you to the audience for watching. You also can ask them to watch your other videos, to comment, or to subscribe to your YouTube channel.

» **Characters:** Every video has characters, whether they're real or made up. If your video uses actors to play characters, think about creating a profile for each character.

» **Emotions:** Audiences like to feel emotions. If you can make your audience laugh, cry, or jump, for example, you've won a great battle. Think of your favorite film. What makes it your favorite? Is it because it makes you feel happy or sad? That's what you want your audience to think about your video.

TIP

A character profile describes the characters in your video. Is he quiet, funny, naughty? Is she smart, grumpy, playful? A character profile helps your actors know how to play their characters.

Watch some other YouTube videos. What works well? What made you laugh or cry? How was the video introduced? How did it end?

SCRIPT YOUR VIDEO

We love writing scripts, because that's the moment a video starts coming to life. Depending on what style you choose, you may want to write a script to explain each scene and create *dialogue* (lines for actors). If you're creating a gaming video, you may want to script parts of the video, like the introduction and ending, or just improvise what you say while you play. Whichever you choose, we would still recommend planning your video as much as you can.

You can see how we wrote and arranged this script.

MILO TOOK MY PHONE

SCENE 1 - NICK'S INTRODUCTION

Action/direction —— Nick is sitting at his desk talking to his webcam. He is holding his phone in his hand.

Character name ——————— NICK
Hi. This is unbelievable! My phone went missing yesterday and I've just found it. When I looked
Dialogue —————— through my phone I couldn't believe what I saw. It appears that Milo, my dog, has taken my phone and filmed himself. Don't believe me? Well, here's what I found!

SCENE 2 - MILO ON SOFA

Milo is lying in his bed and is looking at phone. The phone moves around to make it look like Milo is adjusting the phone to frame himself. Milo's voiceover starts.

MILO VOICEOVER
Right, how do you work this thing... There... Good... Hello. I'm Milo and this is my bed. I lie here most of the day as sleeping is good. Anyway, I took my owners phone and thought I would make a little film about my life. I do hope you enjoy it.

If you're planning to create a short film using a story and lines for your actors, you may want to write a script. The script should have the following parts:

» **Action/direction:** These describe anything happening onscreen besides character dialogue. You can include shot information and notes for filming here, too. Action and direction might explain how an actor behaves or performs his character in a scene. An example of action and direction appears under the first scene heading, where it says, "Nick is sitting at his desk talking to his webcam."

» **Character names:** Stick a character's name before her lines of dialogue so that your actors know who's speaking.

» **Dialogue:** These are the words that you speak or that your characters speak. Make them as natural as possible. For example, in real life you'd say, "I'm sorry. I can't come tonight." Unless you're a superformal person, you wouldn't say, "I am sorry that I cannot come tonight."

Using script software makes writing scripts a lot easier and quicker. It has *templates* (sort of like spaces already made) for arranging the action, character names, and dialogue. That makes the script easier to read.

TIP

We use software called Celtx, which you can download for free from www.celtx.com. Lots of other script writing tools are available, or you can just use a commonly available program, like Word.

Scripting can cut down the number of "ums" and "ers" someone utters. You don't have to write a complete script for your vlog or tutorial, but it does help to make a list of points you want to talk about.

TIP

Plan what you're going to say, even if you're making a vlog or tutorial.

WRITE DIALOGUE

Dialogue is simply a conversation between your characters.

REMEMBER

The key to good dialogue is making it sound natural. Imagine what you'd say if you were the character. And you don't have to use dialogue to explain everything. Use facial expressions, body language, or actions to tell your story.

TIP

Read your dialogue out loud. If you stumble over a word, or if a line is hard to read, look for an easier way to say it.

Dialogue can always change; your actors can say the same thing in their own way. This is okay, as long as the meaning doesn't change.

If you're having trouble thinking of what to write, try acting out your scene or reading aloud what you've already written. You also can ask a friend to help you write the dialogue for your YouTube video.

MAKE A SHOT LIST

Creating a shot list is one of the best things you can do to prepare for filming. Before you film a single thing, list the shots that you want to capture. A *shot list* helps you

» Keep track of what you've filmed

» Plan the location, props, and actors for each shot

TIP

You may use the same location more than once but at different points in your film. For example, maybe you're at a park at the beginning and then at the end of your film. Instead of filming those scenes on different days, film them on the same day.

You can download a blank version of this shot list for your own video, from http://www.dummies.com/go/ makingyoutubevideos2e.

Shot List

Production Title: 'Milo Took My Phone'

Shot No.	Scene No.	Shot Type	Camera Movement	Description
1	1	Mid Shot	Fixed	Webcam shot of Nick at desk
2	6	Mid Shot	Fixed	Webcam shot of Nick at desk
3	2	Close Up	Handheld	Movement to look like Milo is holding camera
4	3	Close Up	Handheld	Movement. Include tilt up to see Nick (not looking at camera)
5	4	Mid Shot	Handheld	Milo's point of view of food
6	4	Close Up	Handheld	Movement to look like Milo is holding camera
7	5	Close Up	Handheld	Movement to look like Milo is holding camera

A shot list has the following information:

» **Shot number** is the number of the shot in the order to be filmed. For example, the first shot you want to film is shot 1, the second is shot 2, and the third is — you get it.

» **Scene number** shows the scene that the shot belongs to. You normally use this when referring to a script from a film with more than one scene. You might not need scene numbers if you're filming a vlog or how-to video. Scene 1 in Nick's video was filmed using a webcam in his study, and he filmed scene 2, Milo in his bed, with an iPhone.

REMEMBER

A film is divided into scenes, which are a series of shots filmed in one location. As soon as the location changes, the scene changes.

» **Shot type** is how close you want to capture your actors. For example, do you want a wide shot, mid shot, or close-up shot? We explain these terms in the next section.

» **Camera movement** is where you choose a fixed-camera position or camera movement. This is explained in more detail later in this project, in the section "Choose Movement or Fixed."

» **Shot description** is where you explain how the shot should look, with any notes to remember when filming. You may want to write notes on the type of camera movement or something you want your actors to do.

CHOOSE A SHOT TYPE

Choosing a shot type refers to how your subject appears on the camera screen or in the viewfinder. By *framing a shot*, you choose what you see through the viewfinder on your camera and what your audience will see when it watches your film.

With gaming, usually the game chooses the best viewing angle or camera shot, but sometimes players can choose their own angles. The next time you play a game, look out for these different angles.

REMEMBER

Take time choosing your shots before you film anything. It saves time on the day of filming because you can get on with shooting rather than decide what shots to use.

» Some filmmakers choose shots before filming.

» Some filmmakers choose shots when they're creating a shot list, which comes after writing the script.

» Some filmmakers choose shots on the day they film, even though there are advantages to choosing shots ahead of time.

Choose your shots before filming. It's less stressful, and the results are usually better.

You have lots of shots to choose from. In the following sections, we explain the different types and when to use them.

WIDE SHOT

A *wide shot,* also known as a *long shot,* shows your audience more of the scene you're filming. Do this by zooming out on your camera or by moving your camera farther away from the subject or character.

Some filmmakers like to start scenes with a wide shot. This *establishing shot* shows more of the location or characters.

You can see that this shot is framed so that the horizontal line follows the line where the grass meets the trees.

Imagine that you want your audience to know that your characters are on a beach. You can begin with a wide shot showing your characters, the sky, the sea, and the sand. Hopefully, no sharks. Instantly, your audience knows where the characters are.

When you're framing a shot, look out for any straight lines you can find, either horizontally (side to side) or vertically (up and down) across the shot. Use these lines to keep your framing straight.

TIP

When should you use a wide shot? Use it in a short film to show your audience the whole scene or when you're filming a funny video starring your pet.

MID SHOT

The *mid shot*, or *medium shot*, frames the characters from a space above their heads to about halfway (*mid*way) down their bodies.

This shot is the most common on TV, film, and YouTube because it shows hand movements, gestures, and facial expressions. You want to capture that stuff.

The mid shot is used a lot in vlogs, reviews, and how tos because it focuses the audience's attention on the upper half of the body.

» A *two shot* is a mid shot used to film two people together. A two shot is often used in TV when two presenters host a show. You can try it in your YouTube videos if you have two characters side by side or face-to-face.

» *Over-the-shoulder shots* are great for conversations between characters who are facing each other. With an over-the-shoulder shot, you see both characters at the same time, but only one character faces the camera.

We like to use over-the-shoulder shots because they let you see the expressions on a character's face. Because the character faces the viewer, these shots can make the audience feel like it's part of the conversation.

You may use an over-the-shoulder shot in your YouTube video if you're interviewing someone or if someone in your short film is having a conversation.

TIP

With over-the-shoulder shots, it's common for actors to look at the camera. That can distract your audience. Move the camera farther away from the actor and then zoom in with the lens.

When should you use a mid shot? When you're filming yourself talking about an interesting topic or doing a review or vlog. Nick used his webcam to capture a mid shot of himself introducing his YouTube video about Milo.

CLOSE-UP

Bringing the camera closer or zooming into your subject or character creates a *close-up shot.*

» A *cut-in* is a close-up shot used to show detail on an object or on a part of the subject that you can already see in the main scene — like a close-up of an actor's hands or of an item an actor is holding.

The scene at the top of the next page shows a cut-in shot of one character passing over a key to another. In this scene, it is important that the audience see the key being passed from one character to another.

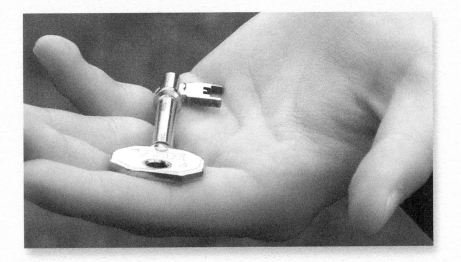

» An *extreme close-up* comes in even closer to your character (right in her mug!) or subject to show even more strong emotion or detail. If you want your audience to know that your character is really angry — hopping mad — you could use an extreme close-up of the actor's face to show the anger in her eyes.

When should you use a close-up shot? How about using a cut-in shot when you're filming a how-to video? Or when you want to show a character's facial expressions to help show emotions? You can use a close-up for any shot that requires more detail. For example, if you want to show the object in your character's hand, use a cut-in to a close-up shot of that object.

CHOOSE MOVEMENT OR FIXED

Besides choosing how to frame your subject, think about whether you're going to mount your camera in a fixed position or move it around.

It's amazing how a small amount of movement from the camera can make a shot look more interesting and help build emotions.

» **Fixed-camera position** is when your camera is locked in one spot, with no movement. Normally for this position, you use a tripod. (See the nearby "Steady does it! Using a tripod" sidebar to read more about it.) If you're creating a tutorial, how-to, or vlog, you may want to use a fixed-camera position with a webcam.

» **Moving camera** means you move your camera during the shot. This might be handheld or on a tripod. If you're filming your pet doing something funny, you might follow it using a camcorder.

REMEMBER

A tripod is like a filmmaker's friend as it can take the weight of the camera while you focus on what you are filming. Most tripods have a moving head (where the camera is attached), which means you can smoothly move the camera left or right (pan) and up and down (tilt), or just keep it still without any movement.

WARNING

Filming a whole video with a handheld (moving) camera can be uncomfortable for the camera operator. Before you choose this approach, be sure it matches the style and mood of your video.

What we love about the art of film is that you can use different types of shots within a scene. An audience seeing a play can watch the stage performance from only one angle. When they're watching film, your audience can see a wide shot, get closer for a mid shot for the dialogue, and then zoom in for a close-up.

STEADY DOES IT! USING A TRIPOD

A tripod is a great tool for

- » Keeping your shots steady
- » Taking the weight of the camera off your camera operator
- » Adding gentle movement to your shots

We like to film some shots on a tripod and some on a handheld because it can change the feeling throughout the video. What you choose depends on what feeling you want. Use a tripod if you want to give the scene a calm or relaxed feel, or if you want the audience to focus on the actors.

You *can* add movement to your shots with a tripod:

Pan shots move your camera horizontally on a tripod from right to left (or from left to right). Don't pan too much within one shot. It can confuse the audience or make them uncomfortable. Don't use more than one pan per shot, if you need to at all.

Tilt shots move your camera vertically (up or down). You may want to use a tilt shot at the beginning of a scene to *establish,* or set up, the location. Too many tilt shots can be uncomfortable too: No more than one per scene.

You can see examples of tilt and pan shots at http://www.dummies.com/go/makingyoutubevideos2e.

If you don't have a tripod, you have other ways of keeping your camera steady, including resting your camera on a table or flat surface, but make sure it's secure and isn't going to fall. If you're using a lightweight camera, you can buy a basic tripod for less than $20. You can also choose from a wide range of low-cost holders, mounts, and tripods for camera phones.

RECORD SOUND

To record sound when filming, you must use a microphone. A *microphone* recognizes noise and changes the sound into data, which is captured by your camera. You can either use the microphone built into the camera or plug an external microphone into your camera.

REMEMBER

The quality — how good something is — of your video sound can be as important as the picture. Poor sound can be distracting and can make your audience decide not to watch your video.

TIP

Spend as much time getting your video's sound right as you do getting its picture right. You'll save time when editing later.

Fixing badly recorded sound in an editing tool is difficult, and in some cases impossible. If the sound is poor or you hear a noise that's impossible to remove, you have to rerecord the sound.

ALL ABOARD WITH THE ONBOARD

An onboard microphone can be useful when you don't have room for an external microphone. A few years ago, Nick filmed a documentary in Ghana, and all he took with him was a camcorder and its onboard microphone. He couldn't use an external microphone, because he was the only member of the film crew and he had to fit all his filming equipment into his carry-on luggage. It was a challenging experience, but it taught him a lot about recording with onboard microphones.

We've had to do this a few times because of noises we didn't notice when filming. A long train whistle over dialogue doesn't work, either.

BUILT-IN MICROPHONE

Because you may have to use a built-in microphone, we explain how to get the best results from one.

WARNING

Nearly all digital camcorders, webcams, and camera phones have built-in microphones called onboard microphones. They're not the best solutions for recording audio or dialogue in videos.

Recording good sound with the onboard microphone on your camera isn't easy, but try using the techniques in the following three sections to get the best possible sound.

GET CLOSE

Sometimes you can't get close, especially if you're shooting a wide shot, but you may be able to use the sound you recorded in the close-up shot or mid shot from the same scene.

WARNING

You can turn up the level of the onboard microphone, but this increases the overall volume, including background noise.

REDUCE CAMERA NOISE

With onboard sound recording, you're more likely to record noise from the camera itself. Such noise may be from the electronics inside the camera, especially when zooming in and out, or it may come from the sounds you make when pressing buttons.

TIP

If you're using the microphone built into your camera, try not to move your hands too much or press buttons when recording. Mounting your camera on a tripod means that you don't have to hold or touch the camera as it's recording, which helps reduce unwanted noises.

REDUCE BACKGROUND NOISE

It isn't easy to control the noises around you, especially if you're filming in a public place, like a park or street. Big-time movie film directors can afford to close roads, but you can't. Or we assume not, anyway.

TIP

Before you start filming, ask the people around you to be quiet for a few minutes so that you can hear background noises. Ask people to keep still, too. Even gentle footsteps may be picked up. Other noise could come from cellphones, landline phones, neighbors, pets, clocks, or passing cars.

You may not have this problem too much if you're filming a vlog or reviewing video in your bedroom, but you may want to warn people in your house that you're filming.

EXTERNAL MICROPHONE

Recording sound with an external microphone can produce better results than an onboard microphone. You can place your camera in one spot and then scoot closer to your subject or character to record sound. Unwanted background noise gets reduced this way, too.

To use an external microphone when filming, have an extra crew member hold the microphone and pay attention to the sound during filming. This extra crew member is the *sound operator*, or *boom operator*.

The external microphone is normally attached to a *boom pole*, which lets the boom operator move the microphone closer to the subject or actor without being in the shot.

WARNING

Your boom operator should be able to hold the boom pole for a long time without dropping it. If the boom operator's arm gets tired, the microphone could appear in the shot.

Ask your boom operator to keep their hands still when holding the boom during filming. The microphone may pick up any tapping or movement on the boom pole.

Some video cameras have a socket on the camera body — either a mini jack or an XLR socket — where you can attach an external microphone using a cable.

Jack input XLR input

When you're recording with an external microphone, try following the techniques in the next three sections to get the best sound.

POINT THE MICROPHONE IN THE DIRECTION OF THE SOUND

External microphones are normally *directional* microphones, which means they pick up sound directly in front of the microphone but not to the sides or behind it. This is good because it will record less background noise.

REMEMBER

When you're using an external microphone, it's important to point the microphone where the sound is coming from. If the microphone is pointing away from the action, it won't record the sound you want.

POSITION THE EXTERNAL MICROPHONE CORRECTLY

You can position the microphone *above* your subject or *below* it. The best position depends on what you're filming:

» **Overhead:** Holding the microphone over the scene is the most common approach. Overhead microphones are better for wider shots and don't pick up noises from your actors' hands or feet.

» **Underneath:** Recording sound from underneath is mainly used when filming mid shots or close-up shots. Go underneath if you have limited room above the actors or to shield the microphone from high winds outside.

AVOID DROPPING THE BOOM IN THE SHOT

A boom pole with an external microphone can feel heavy — especially if you have to hold it during a long scene. Sometimes, the microphone can drop down into the shot, which means you have to stop filming.

TIP

Look out for a boom mic creeping into a shot.

To help prevent the microphone from appearing in your shots, ask your boom operator to rest between takes. When you're not filming, the operator can put the boom pole — the lower end of the pole — on the floor.

WARNING

Don't put the microphone on the ground! It could get damaged.

USE A MICROPHONE FOR DIALOGUE

The keys to recording dialogue: Put the microphone as close to your actor as you can (without the microphone being in the shot) and aim the microphone in the direction of the sound.

TIP

The best way to check for unwanted noises is by wearing headphones. Without headphones, you probably won't hear noise until you're importing the footage into the editing tool. If the sound appears in the background in one shot and not in the next, the sound will be uneven between shots. Your audience will notice.

If you hear a distracting noise — a plane, gust of wind, or passing car — through the headphones when you're filming, stop filming. Wait for the sound to pass, and then retake that shot.

Here are a few ways to avoid unwanted noises during filming:

» **Turn off any air conditioners or fans.** Microphones can pick up noises that sometimes you can't even hear when you're filming.

» **Make sure all cellphones are off.** If you get a call, the shoot has to come to a stop. Sometimes a cellphone's roaming or searching signal can interfere with the camera and wind up on the recorded audio.

» **Don't point the microphone in the direction of any clear background noise.** That includes roads, waterfalls, and fountains. Again, these sounds can come across clearly in the recording and can make it hard to hear dialogue.

» **Don't film in empty rooms.** You'll wind up with lots of echoes in your recording. (But you might *want* echoes in your film.) You can put blankets on walls to help deaden the sound.

DEAL WITH WIND

Boom operators often have wind problems outside. Not *that* kind of wind — the sky kind of wind!

When you're filming outdoors, the microphone may pick up noise from the wind, which can make dialogue hard to hear. If you're not sure what this sounds like, try gently blowing on your camera's microphone and listening through the headphones — it isn't a nice sound.

Camera phones can also suffer from wind noise from the built-in microphone.

Wind noise can only be detected by monitoring the sound using headphones during filming.

REMEMBER

If you can hear wind noise when filming, you need a *windshield*, a furry cover that protects the microphone from the wind. You also can get windshields for onboard microphones on video cameras.

Windshields for external microphones come in different types. (You can see why they're sometimes called *dead cats*.)

A windshield is highly recommended for recording audio outdoors, but if you don't have one, turning your back to the wind and sheltering the camera as much as possible can help.

You can see what external microphones without windshields look like.

If you still have wind noise when filming, try booming from underneath or forming a barrier between the wind and the microphone.

MONITOR SOUND

Monitoring sound is when you listen to the sound being recorded *during* filming. *Checking* sound is when you listen to the sound when watching your footage *after* filming.

REMEMBER

No matter what kind of microphone you're using, monitor (pay attention to) and check the quality of the sound to see if you picked up any unwanted noises or had other issues.

The best way to do this is with a pair of headphones plugged into your camera or recording device. Even better, ask someone to listen and monitor the sound during recording. This way, you can deal with unwanted noises or trouble right away.

Most camcorders have an *audio meter* that lets you see how loud or how low the sound is. The audio meter

normally is on the LCD monitor on your camcorder.
You can use the meter to check sound levels before
filming — make sure that the sound you're recording
isn't so loud that it will distort or isn't so quiet that the
audience won't be able to hear the dialogue.

Some camcorders let you change microphone levels, but
others (including camera phones) do it automatically.
Either way, make sure you monitor the audio levels
before and during filming.

REMEMBER

*Before filming, ask your actors to say some of
their lines as loudly as they would when you're
filming. The bars shouldn't constantly peak (hit
the end of the meter, which is usually red). If a
meter does this, the audio levels are too high.*

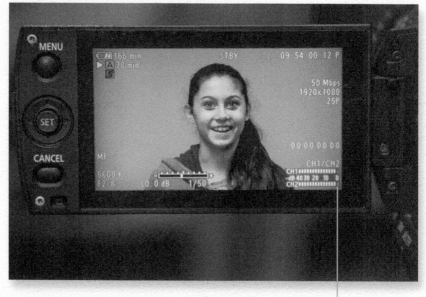

Peaking: the danger zone

If the audio levels are too quiet, on the other hand, the audio meter bars won't rise as much.

Don't worry if your camera has no audio meters. In that case, you can always listen to see whether the audio is too loud or too quiet. By plugging headphones into your camera and listening to the dialogue, you'll be able to hear whether the audio is too loud, because it will distort and be uncomfortable to listen to. On the other hand, if you can hardly hear what your actor is saying, you either need to turn up the microphone volume, move the microphone closer to your actor, or ask the person to speak louder.

DUBBING AND FOLEY

Imagine this: You've had a long day of filming and you return to your edit suite, and whilst reviewing your footage, you notice an unwanted sound on the audio track. What do you do? If the unwanted noise is over dialogue, the options are to either use another recorded take or to rerecord the damaged section of dialogue with the actor and add this in during editing — this is called *dubbing,* which happens frequently on big-budget films and TV shows. Sometimes, whole scenes have to be dubbed because the audio recording was poor.

As we mention earlier, with video, sound is as important as picture, so you may want to add additional sound effects or noises to your video to enhance your audience's experience — these additional sounds are called *foley effects.* You may want to add a door creaking in a scary scene, or the sound of a police siren in a crime drama, or the sound of footsteps on a gravel driveway. All these sounds can be recorded at a later stage and added during the editing process.

LIGHT YOUR VIDEO

Light is important to your YouTube video. Without light, your audience won't be able to see what you've filmed. Light can also help create a mood or affect your audience's feelings. For example, darker shots can make a scene feel scary or sad.

REMEMBER

Video cameras need more light than our eyes do. Most filmmakers use extra lights to help brighten the actors.

USE NATURAL LIGHT

Buying lights for filming can be expensive, but don't worry: You have one of the biggest, most powerful lights available for free — the sun! Sunlight really brightens things up, but as you know, it's only available during the day.

If the sky has just a few (or no) clouds, you have direct sunlight. In that case, you may see more shadows around and on your subject or actor. You can have the actor look directly into the sun, but bright sunlight can make them squint — or burn out their retinas completely.

TIP

You can remove some shadows by using a reflector. It helps bounce light back into the darker areas. Photographers use them too. You might have seen a reflector in action when you had school pictures taken.

You can buy a reflector, or you can use anything that has a large white surface, such as a polystyrene board or large poster board. By angling the reflector toward your subject or actor, the white surface will reflect the sunlight.

Don't film your actors with the sun behind them.

REMEMBER

They'll end up looking shadowy and you might get lens flares, which look like round blobs or streaks of light across your shot. Lens flares can sometimes look great, but they also highlight any dirt or smudges on your camera lens. A cloudy day gives you fewer problems with shadows and lens flares.

You can use daylight to help light scenes in a room (as long as the room has windows). Daylight that's coming through only one window may add shadows to your subject or actor, but you can turn on a lamp or light inside the room.

USE EXTRA LIGHTS

You have to use extra lights anywhere you're filming without sunlight. If your camera is set to automatic and you're filming a scene with low light, the picture quality will be bad. You may end up with a *grainy* image with lots of dots.

This can look good in some shots, but it's not an effect you want to produce accidentally.

TIP

Even if it's an effect you're looking for, it's best to light your video as well as possible and then add effects later, when you're editing.

You may need extra lights if you're filming a vlog or review using your webcam in your room. Professional lights can be expensive, but you can use lights that you already have around. Fitting a good-quality LED bulb for your desk lamp is a good option because they don't get so hot, and you can even get color changing LED bulbs that allow you to choose a color temperature or create a lighting effect.

TIP

What is color temperature? Color temperature has nothing to do with heat, but instead, the color of light. It's measured in Kelvin on a scale from warm (orangey) to cool (bluish). The lamps in your house are likely to be a warmer color, which will measure at around 3200 Kelvin. If you look out the window, daylight will produce a cooler color, which measures at about 5600 Kelvin and higher. Most camcorders, including camera phones, will auto-adjust to the temperature of the light they have around them, a process known as white balancing. More professional cameras will require the operator to set the white balance manually.

TIP

Before you go moving lights around your house, please check with the adult in charge first. You might even ask them to help you.

Nick didn't have any lights when he first started making films, so he used desk lamps. They were great for close-up shots, but usually weren't powerful enough for a wide shot.

The following list describes the types of additional lighting you could use for your video:

» **LED:** You can buy inexpensive LED lights, which are brilliant. Smart, sure. But by *brilliant,* we mean really bright.

We use camera-mounted LED lights with AA batteries. The LEDs are small and lightweight. We sometimes even take the LED lights outdoors while filming.

» **Halogen utility:** You can buy these from hardware stores for a lot less money than professional lighting costs.

WARNING

Halogen utility lights get hot when you use them. Let them cool down before you move them around. They also use a lot of power, so you may want to ask an adult to help you set them up.

REMEMBER

The main thing to remember when lighting your YouTube video is to make sure that every shot looks natural. When the scene in your viewfinder doesn't look natural, something is wrong. Look through the viewfinder. You, your subject, or the actors should look much like they look when you look at them directly, without a camera.

If you're making a vlog, review, or how-to video, shining a desk lamp on your face could provide enough light to make your shot look great. For short films or funny videos that you capture around the house or outdoors, there may be enough light around so that you don't need extra.

Consider these factors when lighting your video:

» **Overexposed shots:** If shots are *overexposed,* it means they're too bright. Some of the brighter areas may have gone white and lost detail. You can see that parts of his face are completely white and that some of the detail and color was lost. It's really hard — usually impossible — to put this detail back with editing.

You can overexpose film by placing too much light on your subject or in your scene, or it can happen because the iris on your camera is open too wide or the aperture is set too low. You can fix this easily by lowering the light or by raising the aperture levels. (You can discover more about aperture in the next section of this project.)

» **Underexposed shots:** If your shots are *underexposed*, they're too dark. You may not be able to see some areas of your subject or actor. You can see only part of the face, and some detail has been lost. Underexposure is easier to repair with editing, but it still isn't great, having to boost the brightness too much. That can affect the color and wind up grainy.

» **Three-point lighting:** This film-and-TV lighting technique has three lights set up around the subject or actor. A three-point lighting setup works like this:

BACK
LIGHT

SUBJECT

KEY
LIGHT

FILL
LIGHT

CAMERA

» The *key light* can be on either side of the subject. It gives the most amount of light to the subject. It brightens one side of the subject's face. (The actual light you see in the figure is just a prop.)

» Put the *fill light* on the opposite side of the key light. It fills in light to make fewer shadows on the face. Set the fill light a little lower in brightness than the key light.

» The *back light* is behind the subject, to one side. It may seem like it doesn't do anything, but it lights around the head to separate the subject from the background.

» If you want to go for it, put all three lights together.

» **Bounced light:** This is our favorite technique because it provides the most natural light. Bounced lighting reflects light off walls, ceilings, and reflectors and onto a subject. Directly shining a light can cast shadows behind a subject or light up a face too much. Bouncing light off the ceiling, wall, or reflector, however, breaks up the light around the room.

Sometimes we use a mixture of bounced light and direct light to get a reflection in an actor's eyes. It can produce a sharper-looking image.

You can combine a key light with bounced light to reflect light in the actor's eyes.

TIP

If you don't have many lights in the room, you can reflect light onto your subject using tinfoil. You can even wrap foil around cardboard to make your own reflector.

APER-WHAT?

Aperture is the hole in the lens that lets light through. The aperture size is controlled by the *iris,* which is a ring that opens and closes inside the lens (to let in more or less light). The lower the aperture number, the wider the hole and the more light coming through. Most camcorders and webcams have an auto-iris function that measures the amount of light in a scene and changes the aperture setting. Some video cameras let you change aperture manually (to whatever you think it should be), but each camera is different. Read your camera's operating manual.

DIRECT YOUR FILM

The *director* works with the actors and crew to get the best from them and make sure the story is being told by what they do.

As a director, it's important to have

» **Good communication skills:** A director usually has in his head an idea what the film should look like. It's your job to get that idea across to the crew and actors. This means you also should be good at communicating and explaining what you want.

» **Confidence:** Directors should be confident about what they want, because the crew and actors need to trust that directors know what they're doing. This includes making decisions. If you want to get an extra shot or refilm something, just do it. We've wasted too many hours wondering whether we should film something. In the time we wasted, we could've just refilmed.

» **Attention to detail:** The director needs to be able to focus on the fine detail of the scene. You have to do many things at once: Watch the actors, know what the camera operator is doing, and listen to the dialogue.

As a director, it's useful to have the following items with you during filming:

» **Director's monitor:** Often, directors watch a TV monitor that's plugged into the camera so that they can see what's happening in the scene.

Don't worry if you don't have one of these monitors. You can direct the scene by looking through the monitor on the camera.

TIP

We think it's easier to watch a scene through a monitor because what the camera sees is normally different from what you see when directly watching a scene. It may sound odd, but your actor's performance can also look very different through a camera.

» **Script:** Having the script with you is a must. With it, you can check the dialogue and keep track of where you are in the scene. We like to make notes on the script to remind us of things to capture and remind ourselves of props or costumes needed for a shot.

» **Storyboard or shot list:** With these items, you can keep track of shots filmed (and those you need to film). We tend to work mainly from the shot list. We can tick off the shots as they're done, plan the day, and see how well we're sticking to the schedule.

When you're directing, imagine the edit in your head as you go. As you film a shot, place it into an imaginary timeline in your head. Picture how the shots go together. It works! And it helps us think of shots we missed or of extra shots and angles. It also helps to imagine how the story is coming together. Is it working? Do you need to change anything?

REMEMBER

You may be worried. There's so much to think about when directing your YouTube video! Don't fret: You'll learn as you go. These things will become natural to you. Plus, we've been directing for many years and we're still learning new things.

DIRECT YOUR ACTORS

The director works with the actors to help them perform the character in the way the writer imagined. Because the actors can't see themselves — they can't see what they look like while they're acting — the director offers advice about how to express emotions and say lines.

WARNING

Be a nice director. You don't want to be harsh and upset your actors. You'll end up with no one to film.

DIRECT YOUR CREW

As a director, it's important to know how the camera works and how to film the types of shots we explain earlier in Project 2. Knowing this stuff helps you explain to your crew how you want your shots to look.

You'll choose shot types that help express a scene's emotion. For example, which shot would you use if you want to show the fear on someone's face? That's right — you'd use a close-up.

USE SHOOTING TIPS

It's exciting to get to the point where you can start filming. Using your script and shot list, you can get your equipment and crew and start.

Before you do, the tips in the next three sections will help get the best from your shoot.

CHECK FOR CONTINUITY MISTAKES

Have you ever watched a film and noticed that the actor picked something up with his left hand, and then in the next shot has it in his right hand? Or have you noticed a glass of soda that's half full, and then in the next shot it's nearly empty? This is a *continuity mistake.*

REMEMBER

Continuity mistakes happen when something in a scene, like a prop or an actor, changes between shots.

Blockbusters normally hire someone to look out for continuity mistakes, but even then they happen. Asking your crew and actors to look out for continuity mistakes will reduce how many happen in your film.

Next time you watch a film, look for continuity mistakes. Keep them to yourself, though. You don't want to annoy the people you're watching with. Otherwise, you might end up watching films on your own, like we do.

ALWAYS GET ONE MORE TAKE THAN YOU NEED

You'll probably film the same shot several times. It takes a bit to get the right take, unless you have a perfect cast and crew. (Spoiler: That's not possible.)

A *take* is one recorded performance in a scene. It starts when the camera operator presses the Record button and stops when they stop recording.

TIP

When you get a good take, you can either go to the next shot on your list or get one more take, to be safe. Get the extra take. Your actors might perform even better, or there might be a mistake in the last take that you didn't notice.

If you're recording a vlog, review, or how-to video, you may want to record a few takes and choose the best one.

SHOOT OUT OF ORDER

Most films are shot out of *sequence,* which means a different order from how they appear in the film. This makes the filming process as simple as possible.

For example, you may want to record all the footage of your cat first and then record your intro. Or maybe film yourself demonstrating a dance before explaining how to do the dance. You're doing the Funky Chicken, right?

CHECK YOUR SHOTS

The last thing you want is to import your footage at the end of the day and find that is has problems and you can't use it. Trust us — we've been there.

REMEMBER

Check your footage after each shot or scene that you film. Make it a habit, even.

BEEN THERE, DONE THAT, GOT THE T-SHIRT

When Nick first started, he filmed a whole day of footage and didn't check the shots after every scene. When he got around to importing the footage onto his computer, he found that there was an issue with the camera and that the footage was no good. He couldn't use any of the shots he filmed that day.

Nick had to arrange the shoot for another day, call the actors and crew back in, and buy them all lunch to say he was sorry. He'll never do that again. He *always* checks the shots after every scene, at least.

Here's why you should check your footage:

» **Technical issues:** You may have a camera issue or dirt on your lens that you didn't notice during filming. Trust us: You'll notice when you play it back on a larger monitor or import it to your computer.

» **Continuity and mistakes:** You may miss mistakes while filming. Maybe an actor stumbled over a word or something shouldn't be in a shot.

» **Missed shots:** Looking through your footage is a great opportunity to double-check that you filmed everything on your shot list.

WARNING

Missing a shot is very easy to do and can cause problems during editing. Check your short list.

Checking your footage is a little more complicated if your camera records with tape instead of media cards.

WARNING

After watching the tape footage, make sure you play to the end of the last take. You don't want to record over any of the scenes you already shot. The safest thing to do is record a placeholder at the end of every scene.

A *placeholder* is just a few seconds of blank video. You might shoot it with the lens cap on. Just be sure you take the cap off for the next shot!

PROJECT 3 EDIT

EDITING IS THE ICING ON THE FILM CAKE. As you edit, you get to see all your footage together, with effects that make for better viewing.

In this project, we show you how to import footage you've captured, cut it together onto a timeline with some cool transitions, and then export it so that it's ready to upload to YouTube.

CHOOSE AN EDITING TOOL

You can choose from tons of editing tools. They offer different effects and work differently, but their basic functions are similar. They allow you to

» Import, or *download,* footage from your camera or media card.

» Cut and arrange video footage on a timeline.

» Add transitions.

» Export what's in your timeline to a final movie.

We cover the process in this project.

REMEMBER

Choosing an editing tool is a lot like choosing a smartphone. Loads of different brands of smartphone are available, and all of them make calls, download apps, browse the Internet, and take photos — though some have more features than others. Also, some people prefer using an iPhone and some prefer using a Samsung, whereas others go for something completely different. When it comes to editing tools, they all edit video for you, but over time you may find that you prefer one tool over another. Our advice to you: Don't settle for the first one you use — try different editing tools to see which one best fits how you work.

This project uses iMovie (for Apple products) and Wondershare Filmora (available for Windows and Apple product operating systems):

» If you have an Apple Macintosh computer or laptop, iMovie is available for free from the App Store.

» Some editing tools can be installed on both Windows and Apple Macintosh computers, including Wondershare Filmora, which is an easy-to-use editing tool with some great features. The free-trial version of Filmora adds a watermark to your video when exporting, which can be removed by paying a small one-off or yearly fee. Check out the discounts for students. The trial and full versions of Filmora can be downloaded from filmora.wondershare.net.

You can buy other editing tools that offer more features and functions, but the tools we just listed offer more than you need for your first YouTube video, and they don't cost anything. You can also choose from a wide range of free editing tools online. An online search will show you these options. (Check out the reviews before downloading any of these tools.)

The HitFilm Express (http://fxhome.com/hitfilm-express) video editing tool not only is free to download and easy to use but also has a user interface (UI) that's quite similar to popular (and expensive) editing software packages, like Adobe Premiere and Apple Final Cut. The advantage with HitFilm Express is that it exports video without a watermark. We use HitFilm Express in Project 4 to edit gameplay footage.

We use Wondershare Filmora and iMovie in this chapter because they both have webcam and voiceover capture features that we use to create our YouTube video.

For a free editing tool with more advanced features, we use Blackmagic DaVinci Resolve, which has been used to edit some well-known feature films. The free version of this software can be downloaded from www.blackmagicdesign.com/products/davinciresolve. (You'll be asked to complete an online form to download this software; please ask a parent or guardian to help with this task.) You can find plenty of good tutorials for this software on YouTube.

Now that all that software talk is out of the way, it's time to actually start a project. First, we show you how to edit your video in iMovie, and then in Filmora. If you have Windows, or if you would rather use Filmora, just skip forward in this project to the section "Import Your Footage into a New Filmora Project."

CREATE A NEW PROJECT IN IMOVIE

We tend to film a new project nearly every day of the year. If all our footage were in one folder, it would be tough to find previous projects and clips.

REMEMBER

Before you start importing your footage to your computer, you need to create a new project. A project is where you can view and arrange your footage onto a timeline to create your final video.

You can create a new project in which to import your footage by following these steps:

1 **Open Applications and click the iMovie icon.**

iMovie opens.

2 **In the iMovie Projects window, choose New Movie from the File menu.**

A new project opens, ready for you to import your footage to edit.

Note that your new project is named My Movie until you save it with a different name, which you can do at a later stage.

My Movie

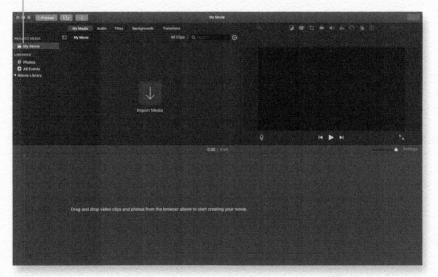

IMPORT YOUR FOOTAGE IN IMOVIE

After you create your project, you can import your video footage into folders called *events*, which appear in the left pane of the iMovie Projects window. When you import video footage into iMovie, it stores your video clips in the iMovie Library on your computer's hard drive.

After you import clips, you can disconnect your camera or remove the media card from your computer.

To import footage, follow these steps:

Connect your camera or device to your computer with a USB cable or FireWire cable.

If you use a media card instead, put it into a media card reader attached to your computer.

1 **If the Import window doesn't automatically appear, click the Import Media icon in the Content Library window or select Import Media from the File menu.**

Your camera, device, or media card should appear in the Cameras/Devices pane (on the left side of the Import window).

2 **Click the name of your card, camera, or device in the Cameras/Devices pane.**

You should see a preview of the first clip. (You can see Milo getting a close-up here.) Under the monitor are thumbnail previews of the video clips on your camera/device.

3 Click the clip(s) you want to import.

4 Select New Event from the Import To drop-down menu at the top of the Import window.

5 Using the dialog box that appears, name your event and click OK.

6 **Click the Import Selected button in the bottom-right corner of the Import dialog box.**

TIP

When the import starts, the Import window closes. You should see your clips in the Event area.

This image shows the iMovie layout.

Event   Footage

Project   Timeline   Playback monitor

RECORD FROM WEBCAM IN IMOVIE

You can record from your webcam directly into your iMovie event by following these steps:

1 **In iMovie, click the Import Media icon or select Import Media from the File menu.**

The Import window appears onscreen.

2 **Click your webcam in the Import window's Camera/ Devices pane.**

You should see a live video preview.

3 **To start recording, click the Record button.**

4 **Do your thing!**

5 **Click the button below the preview monitor again to stop recording.**

6 **Click Close in the bottom-right corner.**

The Import window closes. The clip(s) you just recorded should appear with the other video footage in your new event.

ADD FOOTAGE TO A TIMELINE IN IMOVIE

After your footage is imported into your event, you can edit the footage on the timeline.

REMEMBER

A timeline, or project, is where you drag your footage to edit and place your clips in the correct order.

The great thing about iMovie is that you can easily add clips to your timeline and move them around.

When you're recording footage, you'll have sections, at the beginning and end of the clips, that you don't want to keep. These sections normally include extra material, such as the director shouting orders at actors.

TIP

It might be useful to have your script or shot list in front of you as you edit. This helps you know the order of the clips and ensures that you don't miss any clips.

You can cut off extra bits when you add footage to your timeline. Follow these steps:

1 Make sure your movie project is open.

2 Select from the iMovie Library in the left pane the event that you want to take the footage from.

The footage imported into this event appears in the content browser.

3 Select the first video clip you want to use.

A yellow outline appears around the edge of the selected clip.

Pick the best of the bunch for the first shot in your shot list.

TIP

When you hover the mouse pointer over the footage, you can see a preview in the Playback Monitor dialog box. Select the section of footage you want to use by clicking either edge and dragging to the left or right. The selected footage remains within the yellow outline.

4 **Click and hold in the center of the selected clip, drag your selection down to the beginning of the timeline, and let go.**

Your selected clip appears in the timeline.

5 **Use the controls on the playback monitor to make sure you have all the footage you want.**

The table tells you what each playback control does.

PLAYBACK CONTROLS

Control	What It Does
▶	Plays the footage in the timeline from where the play head is in the timeline. During playback, this turns into the Pause button.
◀|	Takes you back to the beginning of the clip. If you hold it down, the clip rewinds during playback.
▶|	Skips to the next clip in the timeline. If you hold it down, the clip fast-forwards during playback.
⤢	Plays the footage in the timeline in Full Screen mode. Click it again to change it back.

When you play clips, a line moves along the timeline. This line is called the *play head*. You can

» Click the play head and drag it along your timeline.

» Click above a clip to move the play head there.

If you accidentally cut off part of the video at the beginning or end, you can always bring it back by extending the clip in the timeline.

6 **Select the clip that you want to extend or shorten, and hover the mouse pointer over the beginning or end of the clip.**

The cursor changes to two arrows pointing away from each other. Click and hold, and then move the cursor left or right.

7 To add your second shot, select the footage you want and then follow the same steps for adding your first clip.

Sometimes it's hard to get those two arrows to appear in the play head. Be patient.

TIP

8 Click and drag the shot to the right of your first clip in the timeline, and then let go.

This step automatically places your second shot after your first.

9 Repeat this step again and place the shot to the right side of the second shot.

10 Keep adding clips to your timeline in the order on your shot list.

If you need to swap one clip with another, click and drag the clip where you want it, and then let go.

TIP

11 To remove sound from a video clip, hover the mouse pointer over the line between the video and audio sections within the clip.

The cursor should turn into two arrows, one pointing up and one pointing down.

12 Click and drag the line to the bottom of the clip.

The table lists some keyboard shortcuts that can help with editing.

KEYBOARD SHORTCUTS

Keyboard Shortcut	What It Does
Command-I	Imports footage into an event
Spacebar	Plays the video in the timeline from where the play head is
Right-arrow key	Moves the play head one frame forward, which helps with precise editing
Left-arrow key	Moves the play head one frame backward, which helps with precise editing
Down-arrow key	Jumps play head to the beginning of the next clip in the event browser or timeline
Up-arrow key	Jumps play head to the beginning of the current clip or previous clip in the event browser or timeline

Keyboard Shortcut	What It Does
Forward slash (/)	Plays the selected area of the clip in the event browser or timeline
Backslash (\)	Plays from the beginning of the clip, event, or timeline
Shift-Command-F	Plays the clip from the play head position in Full Screen mode
Esc	Exits Full Screen mode
Command-Z	Undoes the last action or change
Shift-Command-Z	Redoes the last action or change
Command-C	Copies the selected clip or text
Command-X	Cuts the selected clip or text
Command-V	Pastes the copied clip or text

ADD TRANSITIONS IN IMOVIE

With your video footage in the timeline, think about how one video clip joins another. That's a *transition*. A transition can be anything from a simple hard cut to a bit of flashy animation, depending on the type of YouTube video you're creating.

iMovie offers certain kinds of transitions, so add one at the beginning and ending of your video by following these steps:

1 **Choose the** Transitions **tab above the content browser.**

2 **Click and drag the transition you want to the beginning of your first clip in the timeline, and then let go.**

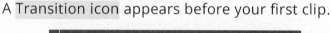 A Transition icon appears before your first clip.

3 **Click and drag the transition to the end of the last clip on the timeline. Then let go.**

You can see what all this looks like by moving the play head to the beginning of the timeline and clicking the Play button under the playback monitor.

WARNING

Use transitions carefully. Using too many can make your video feel long and not professional. Transitions usually show time passing or help change the mood. Using crazy transitions like Mosaic or Spin Out can distract your audience, which isn't a good idea. Keep it simple. Films and TV shows normally use just a few types, like fades and cuts.

ADD JUMP CUTS IN IMOVIE

Unwanted footage might show someone thinking of a line or stumbling over a word. Jump cuts are popular, and filmmakers often use them even if there isn't much to cut out.

REMEMBER

Jump cuts are simply hard transitions that shorten a video or eliminate any unwanted footage. Jump cuts are common in YouTube videos, especially vlogs and tutorials.

To add jump cuts to your YouTube video timeline, follow these steps:

1 **Make sure your project timeline is open.**

2 **Find a section of video in your timeline that you want to get rid of.**

3 **Click in the timeline where you want to start cutting.**

The play head moves to this point in the timeline.

4   **On the keyboard, press Cmd and then the B key.**

The clip splits.

5   **Click in the timeline where you want to stop cutting.**

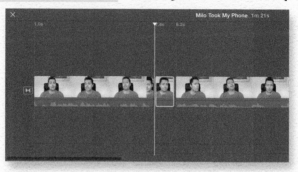

6   **On the keyboard, press Cmd and then B.**

7   **Select the section of footage you want to ditch. On the keyboard, press Delete or Backspace.**

The unwanted footage is removed. Take a look at the video in the timeline to see what your jump cut looks like.

ADD TITLES IN IMOVIE

Titles are words that appear over the footage in a video and give the audience information. Most titles are at the beginning of a video, and they tell the name of the video and information about the filmmakers. (Hey, that's you!)

You can add titles over video or over a blank screen before the clips or anywhere in your timeline.

For now, start by adding a title at the beginning of your YouTube video:

1 **Click the Titles tab above the content browser.**

2 **You see a list of titles. To see what the titles look like, click at the beginning of the title thumbnail and press the spacebar.**

3 **When you find the title you want to use, click and drag the title to the start of your timeline.**

We chose the title *Expand*. When you've dragged the title into the timeline, the preview monitor shows your title with Title Text Here highlighted.

TIP

Choose a title effect that suits your YouTube video style. Also, choose the right amount of time to display it. Read your title out loud slowly. That's how long it should play.

If your video is a vlog or tutorial, you may not want a flashy effect. Also think about how long your title plays. Don't make it so short that your audience doesn't have time to read it. (But don't make it so long that your audience gets bored.)

4 **Double-click the title in the preview monitor to enter your text.**

5 **Select a font from the Font drop-down list above the Title preview window.**

A *font* is the way words, numbers, and symbols look.

6 **To change the size of the font, select the text in the title box, click the** text size drop-down menu, **then select a size.**

7 **Watch the title in your video by clicking at the start of your timeline and pressing the spacebar.**

RECORD A VOICEOVER IN IMOVIE

You may want to use a voiceover as part of your YouTube video. As long as you have a microphone or webcam connected to your computer, iMovie's tool for recording voiceovers will work for you.

Before recording your voiceover, keep in mind these simple ways to improve the quality of the audio recording:

» **Make sure it's as quiet as possible around you.** You may want to let people know that you're recording audio.

» **Check for echoes.** Clap or say a word loudly. Then listen carefully for any echo. If you hear one, try another room. A room with carpeting or lots of rugs and sofas is a good bet.

>> **Position your mouth about seven inches away from the microphone.** That's about from the end of your thumb to the end of your outstretched little finger. Extend that pinky!

To record the voiceover using iMovie, follow these steps:

1 **Have your voiceover script ready to read.**

Move the play head to the point in your timeline where you want to start your voiceover.

2 **On your keyboard, press the V key.**

The voiceover recording function opens. If it doesn't open, click Record Voiceover from iMovie's Window menu.

3 **Click the Record icon (red circle) to start recording your voiceover.**

A countdown gives you three seconds before recording. After that, start your voiceover.

Because you're recording, a red-and-green strip appears underneath your footage.

4 **Click the Stop icon to stop recording.**

A voiceover appears below your footage in a green Audio box, and the voiceover clip appears as an audio clip in your event. You can trim the beginning and ending of your voiceover.

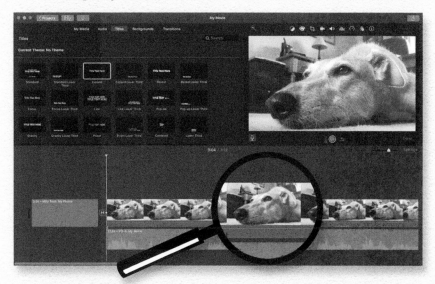

5 **To trim your voiceover, select it. Then hover the mouse pointer over the beginning or ending of the clip.**

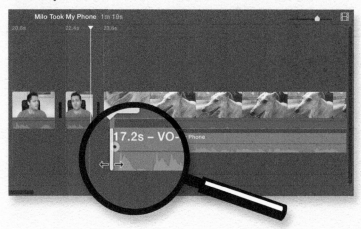

6 **When two arrows appear, click and drag left or right to make the clip shorter or longer.**

You can't make a clip longer unless you already trimmed to make it shorter.

REMEMBER

If you want to record another voiceover in your timeline, repeat these steps.

IMPORT YOUR FOOTAGE INTO A NEW FILMORA PROJECT

Before opening Filmora, you need to set up a folder for the footage on your computer. You don't want to be editing your footage stored on your camera or device.

A project is the area of the editing tool where you import and arrange your footage.

REMEMBER

To import video footage into your project, follow these steps:

1 **Import the footage from your card, camera, or device into the folder you created on your PC.**

Some cameras come with software (on a DVD) that lets you download the footage from the camera to your computer. You can find the same software on the device maker's website.

2 **Open Filmora from Apps.**

3 **Select New Project.**

The Filmora Message Center window may appear. You can close this window for now.

4 **Click the** Import Media Files Here **link.**

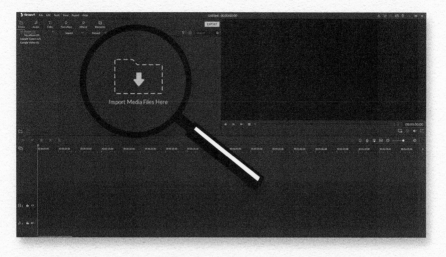

5 **Navigate to the folder where your video footage is stored on your computer.**

Each take or clip recorded by your video camera will appear as a separate file. Your camera normally names the files, using some seemingly random numbers, so they may not make sense.

6 **Click to select the file(s) you want and then click Open.**

The files you select appear in your project timeline as thumbnails (small pictures).

TIP

You can choose more than one file by holding down the Ctrl key on your keyboard and clicking the files in the browser.

7 **Choose File ⇨ Save Project As from the main menu.**

8 **Go to the folder where you want to save your project, type a name, and then click Save.**

We like to save our projects in the same folder as the video footage.

WARNING

Save your project often. You never know when Filmora might crash, losing all your hard work. If you want to be lazy, you can just press Ctrl+S on your keyboard to save your project.

This image shows the Filmora workspace layout.

Content Folders | Content Browser | Timeline | Preview monitor

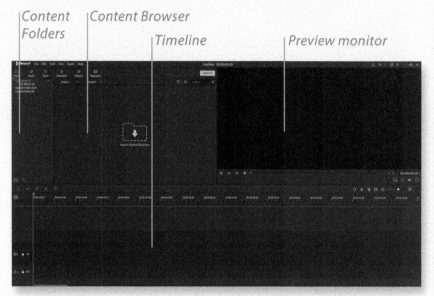

RECORD FROM A WEBCAM IN FILMORA

You can record from your webcam directly into your Filmora project by following these steps:

1 In Filmora, click the Record drop-down menu button above the footage browser.

A drop-down list appears.

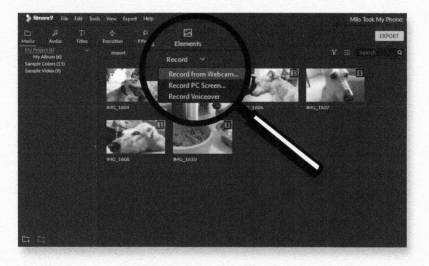

2 Select the Record from Webcam option.

The Capture Video window opens and you should see a live video preview of your webcam. If you don't, you should be able to select your webcam from the Video Device drop-down menu.

3 To start recording, click the Camera icon or press the spacebar.

A countdown appears — three seconds to get ready!

4 **Do your thing!**

5 **Click the button below the preview monitor again to stop recording.**

6 **Click OK in the bottom-right corner.**

The Capture Video window closes. The clip(s) you just recorded should appear with your other video footage in your footage browser.

ADD FOOTAGE TO A TIMELINE IN FILMORA

After you've imported footage into your Filmora project, you can edit it using Filmora's timeline.

REMEMBER

A timeline, or project, is where you drag your footage to edit and place your clips into the right order.

The great thing about Filmora is that you can easily add clips to your timeline and move them around.

When you're recording your footage, you'll have sections at the beginning and end of the clips that you don't want to keep. These sections normally include extra material, such as the director shouting orders at actors.

TIP

It might be useful to have your script or shot list in front of you as you edit. This helps you know the order of the clips and ensures that you don't miss any clips.

You can cut off extra bits when you add your footage to your timeline. Follow these steps:

1 Make sure that your movie project is open and that you can see your imported footage in the content browser.

If you can't see your footage, make sure the Media tab in the upper left corner of the Filmora main window is selected.

2 Double-click on the first video clip you want to use in the footage browser.

3 Choose the best of the bunch for the first shot in your shot list.

TIP

When you double-click on a video clip, you can see a preview in the playback monitor. Select the section of footage you want to use by pressing the I key (which stands for In) at the point you want your clip to start, and then pressing the O key (which stands for Out) at the point you want your clip to end. You'll notice that markers appear below the playback monitor, indicating the In and Out points on your clip. The selected footage lies between these points.

You can use the playback controls to start, stop, and skip through frames to help you find the right In and Out points on your clip. You can also use the spacebar as a toggle to play and pause your video, and press the left- and right-arrow keys to skip frames backward and forward.

4 **Click and hold in the center of the selected clip in the footage browser, drag your selection to the beginning of the timeline, and then let go.**

Your clip selection appears in the timeline.

A dialog box may appear, asking whether you want to change the project settings to match your clip. Click the Match to Media button to change your project settings.

5 **Use the controls on the playback monitor to make sure you have all the footage you want.**

When you play your clips, a line moves along the timeline. This line is called the *play head*. You can

» Click the play head and drag it along your timeline.

» Click above a section in the clip to move the play head to that section.

If you accidentally cut off part of the video at the beginning or end, in the timeline you can easily bring back what you've lost.

6 **Select the clip that you want to extend or shorten, and hover** the mouse pointer **over the beginning or end of the clip.**

The cursor changes to two arrows, pointing away from each other.

7 **Click and hold, and then move the cursor left or right to remove footage or bring back the footage you edited out.**

Sometimes it's hard to get those two arrows to appear in the play head. Be patient.

TIP

8 **To add your second shot, double click on the clip you want from the content browser.**

9 **Use the same steps you used on your first clip to set the in and out points.**

10 **Click and drag the** shot to the right of your first clip **in the timeline. Then let go.**

This step places your second shot after your first.

If the two clips in the timeline aren't touching, you see a small section of black video between them.

TIP

11 Repeat this step again and place your next shot to the right side of the second clip.

12 Keep adding clips to your timeline in the order on your shot list.

TIP

You can use different video tracks, or layers, if you want to overlay footage over other clips or if you need to move clips around the timeline. This can be done by either dragging a new clip onto the existing second video layer or dragging a clip from the first video layer to the second.

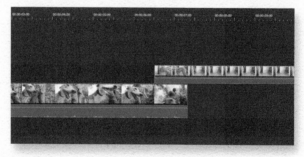

13 **To remove sound from a video clip, hover the mouse pointer over the line between the video and audio sections within the clip on the timeline.**

The cursor should turn into the shape of a hand, and the volume level appears.

14 **Click and drag the volume level line to the bottom of the clip.**

ADD TRANSITIONS IN FILMORA

When you have your clips where you want them to appear on YouTube, you can add transitions.

A *transition* is how one video clip joins another. A transition can be anything from a simple hard cut to a bit of flashy animation, depending on the type of video you're creating.

You can add Filmora transitions to the footage in your project timeline like this:

1 **Click the Transition tab in the bar above the content browser.**

You see different transitions appear in the content browser with a list of styles in the left pane.

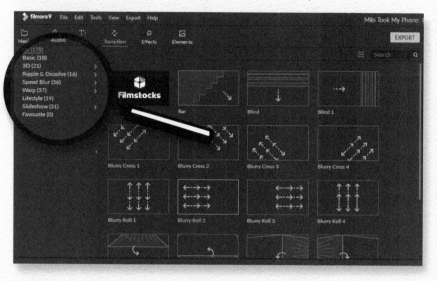

TIP

You can double-click on a transition to see how it works. You can find some fun transitions there.

2 **Click and drag the transition you want to the beginning of your first clip in the timeline. Then let go.**

We're adding a fade at the beginning and end of our video.

A Transition marker appears over the beginning of your first clip.

3 **Click and drag the transition to the end of the last clip on the timeline. Then let go.**

You can see what all this looks like by moving the play head to the beginning of the timeline and clicking the Play button under the playback monitor.

Use transitions carefully. Using too many can make your video feel long and less than professional. Transitions usually show time passing or help change the mood. Using crazy-looking transitions like Mosaic or Spin Out can distract your audience, which isn't a good idea. Keep it simple. Films and TV shows normally use just a few types, like fades and cuts.

ADD JUMP CUTS IN FILMORA

Unwanted footage might show someone pausing to think of their next spoken line or stumbling over a word. Jump cuts are popular, and filmmakers often use them, even if there isn't much to cut out.

REMEMBER

Jump cuts are simply hard transitions that shorten a video or cut out any unwanted footage. Jump cuts are common in YouTube videos, especially vlogs and tutorials.

1 Find a section of video in your timeline to get rid of.

Click in the timeline where you want to start cutting.

The play head moves to this point in the timeline.

2 **On the keyboard, press Ctrl and then the B key.**

The clip splits.

3 **Click in the timeline where you want to stop cutting.**

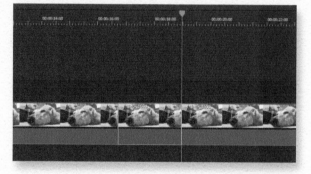

4 **On the keyboard, press Cmd and then the B key.**

5 **Select the section of footage you want to ditch. On the keyboard, press Delete.**

You see a gap of black video where the removed clip was. You can close this gap.

6 **Select the area of the timeline with no video and press Delete on the keyboard.**

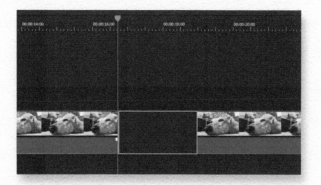

The unwanted footage is removed. Take a look at the video in the timeline to see what your jump cut looks like.

ADD TITLES IN FILMORA

Titles are words that appear over the footage in a video and give the audience information. Most titles are at the beginning of a video, and they tell the name of the video and information about the filmmakers. (Hey, that's you!)

You can add titles over video, or over a blank screen before the clips, or anywhere in your timeline.

For now, start by adding a title at the beginning of your video:

1 **Click the Titles tab in the bar above the content browser.**

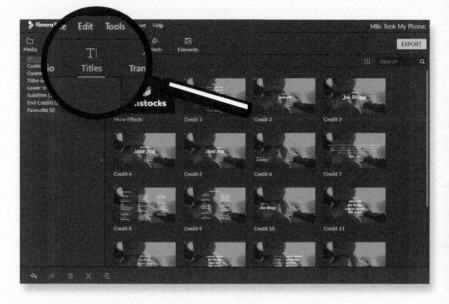

You see the different titles appear in the content browser with a list of title styles in the left pane. To see what the titles look like, double-click on the title thumbnail.

2 **When you find the title you want to use, click and drag the title onto an empty video track at the start of your timeline.**

This step overlays the title on your footage. If you want your title to appear before your footage starts, you can move all your footage along the timeline by pressing Ctrl and A on the keyboard to select all the footage and then clicking and dragging your first clip to the point you now want it to start.

We chose a simple title to start our video. When you've dragged the title into the timeline, the preview monitor shows your title with *Lorem Ipsum* highlighted (this is called *placeholder* text).

Choose a title effect that suits your YouTube video style. Also, choose the right amount of time to display it. Read your title out loud slowly. That's how long it should play.

3 Double-click on the title in the timeline to show the Editor window.

You can select which title line to edit in the playback monitor and enter your own title in the Editor window.

4 Select a font from the list.

A font is the way words, numbers, and symbols look.

5 To change its size, click the text size drop-down menu **and select the size you want.**

You can explore lots more text editing options here.

6 When you're happy with your title, click OK.

Watch the title in your video by clicking at the start of your timeline and pressing the spacebar on your keyboard.

RECORD A VOICEOVER IN FILMORA

You may want to use a voiceover as part of your YouTube video. As long as you have a microphone or webcam connected to your computer, Filmora's tool for recording voiceovers will work for you.

Before recording your voiceover, keep in mind these simple ways to improve the quality of the audio recording:

» **Make sure it's as quiet as possible around you.** You may want to let people know that you're recording audio.

» **Check for echoes.** Clap or say a word loudly. Then listen carefully for any echo. If there is one, try another room. A room with carpeting or lots of rugs or sofas is a good bet.

» **Position your mouth about seven inches away from the microphone.** That's about from the end of your thumb to the end of your outstretched little finger. Extend that pinky!

To record the voiceover using Filmora, follow these steps:

1 **Have your voiceover script ready to read.**

2 **Move the play head on the timeline where you want to start your voiceover.**

3 **Click the Media tab in the bar above the content browser.**

4 **Click on the arrow next to Record and select Record Voiceover from the drop-down menu that appears.**

5 **Click the Red Microphone icon to start your voiceover.**

A countdown appears — three seconds to get ready! The video will start recording.

6 **Do your thing!**

7 **Click the red Stop icon to quit recording.**

Your voiceover appears below the footage in the timeline and in the content browser.

8 **Click OK when you have finished recording your voiceover.**

You can trim the beginning and ending of your voiceover.

9 **To trim your voiceover, select it in the timeline. Then hover the mouse pointer over the beginning or ending of the clip.**

10 **When two arrows appear, click and drag left or right to make the clip shorter or longer.**

REMEMBER

You can't make a clip longer unless you already trimmed to make it shorter.

If you want to record another voiceover in your timeline, repeat these steps.

WHAT'S MORE FUN THAN PLAYING VIDEOGAMES? MAKING A GAMING YOUTUBE VIDEO! In this chapter, we use HitFilm Express to edit gameplay. HitFilm Express is a fantastic, free editing tool with some great features; you download it from http://fxhome.com/hitfilm-express.

REMEMBER

Before downloading HitFilm Express, you're asked to share a post on social media. If you're under 13, please ask a parent or guardian to help you with this.

IF HITFILM IS FREE, WHAT'S ALL THIS ON THE LEFT?

When you launch HitFilm Express, a massive window fills your computer screen with an array of options, including some that have a fee associated with them. The features listed on the left side are features that, while cool (3D effects and advanced visual effects, for example), are not essential in basic video editing. You can always download them later, if you want to try them, and HitFilm provides plenty of tutorials on how these advanced features can work for future video projects.

In this project, we show you how to edit and export your project in HitFilm Express and upload your video to YouTube. Before you can do that, though, we have to walk you through capturing your game footage. There are options that are unique for each gaming platform, so in this chapter we show you how to do this on PlayStation, Xbox, Windows, and Macintosh.

CAPTURING GAME FOOTAGE FROM A PS4

Capturing gameplay from Sony's PlayStation is supereasy. Make sure you have your controller handy and an external USB drive — you'll need the drive to get the footage off the console.

REMEMBER

Before playing your game, navigate on the PlayStation menu to the Sharing and Broadcasts section, and then select Video Clip Settings from the options offered. The Length of the Video Clip option allows you to set how long of a capture you want to make. Though the 10 Minutes setting lets you capture more of a variety of clips, longer settings like 30 Minutes and 60 Minutes may capture moments of awesomeness you might have missed while playing. Also make sure you've set the Dimensions option to 1920 x 1080.

Video Clip Settings

Length of Video Clip
The resolution and quality of recorded video might cause the length of video clips to be shorter than the length you set here.

30 Seconds
1 Minute
3 Minutes
5 Minutes
10 Minutes
15 Minutes
30 Minutes
✓ 60 Minutes

⊗ Enter   ○ Back

Follow these steps to capture gameplay on your PS4:

1 **After finishing the gameplay you want to share on YouTube, hit the Share button located in the upper left of your controller.**

A Share menu appears onscreen.

2 **Either scroll down to the Save Video Clip option or simply press the purple square on your controller.**

The gameplay clip can be accessed by going back to the PlayStation main menu and accessing the Capture gallery.

3 **Connect a removable USB storage device to your PS4.**

4 **Go to the Capture gallery and find the game you want to share. In that game's gallery, highlight the video clip you want to share, and then press the Options button in the upper right of your controller.**

5 From the listed options, choose **Copy to USB Storage Device** and follow the onscreen steps to copy the clip to your external device.

Depending on the amount of time you captured, this step may take a few minutes.

6 Repeat Steps 4 and 5 for other clips you want to copy to your USB drive.

If your video clips are long, they will take up considerably more space than shorter clips.

REMEMBER

7 When you have all your clips collected, disconnect your USB drive.

CAPTURING GAME FOOTAGE FROM AN XBOX ONE

The process of capturing gameplay from Microsoft's XBox One is similar to capturing gameplay from the PlayStation. Again, have your controller and an external USB drive at the ready.

Follow these steps to capture gameplay on your XBox One:

1 **Connect a removable USB storage device to your Xbox.**

2 **Press the XBox button in the center of your controller to open the Guide.**

3 **Go to the System section on the menu that appears and select the Settings option.**

4 **Go into Preferences and select the Broadcast & Capture option.**

5 **Choose the Capture Location option and then select your external device.**

6 **After finishing the gameplay you want to share on YouTube, go to your XBox controller and press the XBox button, located at the center, to open the Guide menu.**

7 **Choose the View option, select Capture What Happened, and then specify the amount of time you want to capture.**

Your clip is stored in the location you chose in Step # 5.

You can also capture with the XBox in real time by pressing the XBox button on your controller, choosing the View option, and then selecting Record from Now to start recording.

8 **When you have all your clips collected, disconnect your USB drive.**

CAPTURING GAME FOOTAGE FROM A PC OR MACINTOSH

If you're gaming on a computer running Windows or Macintosh, you need to use screen capture software. We use Open Broadcaster Software (https://obsproject.com) or OBS, which is often associated with streaming video but can also be used to capture gameplay on your computer. This software is a free, safe download and is easy to use after you set it up.

Download OBS and follow the installation steps to get OBS running on your computer, and then follow these steps to capture gameplay on your Windows or Macintosh:

1 **Set up your gameplay as you want it — audio, video, webcams — and then launch your game.**

2 **Launch OBS and click the Settings button. Select the Output tab and choose the Mp4 option from the Recording Format drop-down menu in the Recording section.**

Either leave as is the default location of where your captures are kept or set up a new device in the Recording Path section.

3 **Click OK in the bottom right.**

4 **In the Scenes pane in the lower left of the main OBS window, create a new scene by pressing the Plus Sign (+) icon and calling it Game Capture.**

5 **Click OK.**

6 **In the Sources pane to the right of the Scenes pane, create a new source by pressing the Plus Sign (+) icon and selecting Display Capture from the options provided.**

7 **In the new window provided under the Create New option, either leave your display capture labeled as is or call it Gameplay or the name of the game you're intending to capture. (The Make Source Visible option should be selected.)**

Display Capture captures whatever is on your screen. If you have one monitor, you see an *infinity screen* in the preview monitor, showing a screen within a screen within another screen and so on forever. That's normal. (When you actually start the game, you'll record only one screen.) This is Display 0, as shown on the Display menu. If your computer gaming setup has more than one monitor, select the display you want to capture in this window.

If you can afford one, a second monitor will benefit you in your gameplay recording. It doesn't have to be as advanced or as large in resolution as your gameplay monitor, but it does help.

TIP

8 **Click OK.**

If you can't see all of your screen in the Record monitor, you may need to resize the capture area in the Record Monitor. All this depends on your computer's screen resolution.

REMEMBER

9 Click the Start Recording button in the Controls pane in the lower right of the main OBS window.

10 Return to your video game (in Full Screen mode) and begin gameplay.

11 When you finish your gaming session, return to the OBS main window and click the Stop Recording button in the Controls pane.

Your video is now saved with a date stamp as its title in the folder or on the device you have designated in the OBS' Recording Path option in Settings.

REMEMBER

After you set up OBS, you don't need to repeat Steps 1–4. If, however, OBS doesn't remember your settings, feel free to repeat Setup from the beginning.

WARNING

When capturing directly from your PC or Mac, you might notice that gameplay may not look as smooth as when you're playing the game. Also, depending on the resolution you're able to capture in, you may encounter problems when editing the video. All this has to do with your installed graphics card: All video gameplay is sent through a graphics card, and if your graphics card lacks the ability to handle processing gameplay and capturing the game in real-time, the quality of the recording won't be as high as you may expect.

IMPORTING GAMEPLAY INTO HITFILM EXPRESS

After you have your gameplay captured, it's time to work on it using HitFilm Express. Let's assume that you have all of your gameplay on an external hard drive.

Plug the device holding your gameplay into your video editing computer and get ready to do some editing:

1 **Launch HitFilm Express.**

2 **Choose File ➪ New from the main menu to begin your new project, and then click OK to enter the work area.**

3 **In New Project Settings, select the Template setting that best matches your captured game footage.**

YouTube supports resolutions up to 4K and frame rates up to 60fps. We've selected the 1080p Full HD @ 30fps option from the Template drop-down menu, which is the setting we used when capturing the footage. If you're gaming from a PC, check the capture settings in OBS and set your HitFilm project settings to match.

Note that your HitFilm workspace should be divided into six areas:

» **Media:** When you import media (images, video, audio), it appears in this window.

» **Trimmer:** This pane shows the selected video in the Media pane. You can make simple edits here, such as setting the In (start) and Out (end) points of your gameplay clips.

» **Viewer:** This preview monitor allows you to view your clips and edited project.

» **Effects:** This is where you find *transitions,* which add a little polish to your project.

» **Editor:** On this timeline, you place clips in the order you want them to play and then add transitions as well as different effects.

» **Meters:** Audio output is monitored here.

TIP

If, on launching HitFilm Express, your workspace layout has changed or you close a panel by accident, simply choose View–Workspaces–Editing from the main menu, and the workspace will reset to the default editing layout.

4 **In the Media pane, click Import, navigate to wherever your gameplay is stored, select the clip you want to import into the project, and then click the Open button.**

The Media pane should be in the upper left of the main window.

5 **Repeat Step 4 until you have imported all the media you want.**

As part of this project, why don't you import some still screen captures from your game to use as your video introduction? In this project, we're using an image called LoW − PC.jpg for the example.

BASIC EDITING IN HITFILM EXPRESS

Your gameplay is now imported into HitFilm Express, so let's get to editing! Start by creating a basic introduction to your video:

1 **Click-and-drag a still image of gameplay that you've imported to the Editor window, placing it on the Video 2 track.**

If you want to make an image run longer than the default 5 seconds, place the cursor at the end of a clip until a green bracket appears, and then click-and-drag it to the length you want it to run. (For example, we dragged the image's Out point to a new duration of 8 seconds.)

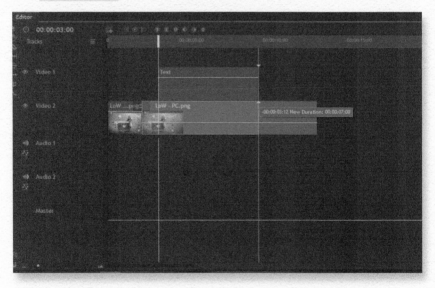

2 In the Editor window, locate the white timeline playhead, and then click-and-drag it to the 2-second mark of the project.

3 Select the Slice tool from the set of editing tools on the left side of the Editor window.

4 **Place the cursor back on the white line extending from the timeline marker at the 2-second mark. When it turns red, click the clip so that it's now in two sections.**

5 **Click the Select tool — it looks like an arrow pointing northwest — and then move the cursor to the rightmost section of the clip you just split, placing it on the white line cutting across the top.**

The cursor should turn into an arrow pointing up and down. This is an Opacity tool, allowing you to make an image darker or transparent.

6 **Click-and-drag the opacity level to 50.00, or as close to that number as you can.**

The Opacity tool allows you to fade images or video on top of one another, but because there's no other media above or below your introduction image, HitFilm Express uses its Black Video effect, making the image darker.

7 **In the Effects pane**, click the arrow next to Transitions — Video to expand the Video Transition options.

8 **After expanding your Video Transition options, open the Dissolve folder, find the Cross Dissolve transition, and then click-and-drag it on top of the cut between the two clips.**

The green box representing the transition should extend before and after the cut.

9 **After making sure the timeline playhead is at the beginning of the project, go to the Viewer window and press the spacebar.**

As the introduction plays, you'll notice that the image dims slightly. In that darker section, you can add a title. Here's how:

10 **Drag your timeline playhead to the 3-second mark.**

11 **In the Viewer pane, select the Text tool and then type a title for your video project.**

For this project, we typed A Guardian's Hits and Misses: Destiny 2 Gameplay.

Text tool

You can edit the appearance of your text by selecting sections of your title and then adjusting the font, size, and other settings in the Text pane — one of the tabs grouped with the Effects pane.

12 **Drag the Out point of your introduction image to match the end of your Text clip.**

13 Back in the Effects pane, click to select the Effects tab, and then click-and-drag a Cross Dissolve transition to the beginning of the Text clip.

This step should have your text fading in at the beginning. Repeat Step 9 to review any changes you've made.

14 Choose File ⇨ Save from the main menu to save your video project.

If it's the first time you're saving the project, you need to name your project and specify a save location.

TIP

Save and save often, in case of any unexpected crashes.

MORE BASIC EDITING IN HITFILM EXPRESS

You now have an introduction to your video, but now you need to get to the actual gameplay itself:

1 Click-and-drag the timeline playhead to the end of your introduction clip.

This is where you'll place the first gameplay clip.

2 From the Media pane, select one of your imported media files.

You should see the video appear in the Trimmer pane.

3 **Using the Trimmer's horizontal scroll bar (the "Scrubber" tool), find the exact point where you want to start your clip and then press the I key, setting an In point for this clip.**

There's a good possibility your gameplay clips are lots longer than you need, but you can use the Trimmer to set In and Out points in your clips, saving yourself a little bit of time in cutting unwanted video.

TIP

Always shoot more footage than you need. Not capturing enough footage makes editing a lot harder.

4 **Move the scrubber to the point where you want your clip to end and then press the O key, setting an Out point.**

5 **Click-and-drag the clip in the Trimmer window to the Video 2 track in the Editor window. Let the clip snap to wherever you placed the timeline playhead.**

A green box representing audio and video gets placed in the project.

Because of the nice work we did in setting the In and Out points in the Trimming pane in Steps 3 and 4, we don't have to deal with the hassle of dropping in a 30-second clip and trimming it in the Editor window.

6 **Return to the Effects pane, find a Cross Dissolve transition in the Transitions — Video folder, and then click-and-drag it to wherever the introduction image and the first gameplay video meet.**

7 **Still in the Effects pane, look for the Transitions — Audio folder. (It's just above the Transitions — Video folder.) Select the Fade transition from that folder, and then click-and-drag it to the beginning of the gameplay's audio track.**

An audio Fade transition slowly brings up the sound level, making the transition from silence to gameplay smoother. (If you want to know what we mean, try listening to the audio without the transition, and then with the transition. You should notice the difference.)

8 Repeat Steps 2–7 to add more clips to your video project.

REMEMBER

You can change the start and end points of your clips in your editor by clicking at the beginning or end of each clip and dragging to the left or right.

RESOLVING RESOLUTION

Resolution settings can be a tricky business. As you can see in the Before image, the video isn't filling the screen in the Viewer pane. That's because the Trimmer is showing the actual video clip, and the viewer is showing the project as it will appear when exported. The settings for the viewer are at 1920 x 1080 pixels, but this clip is at 1280 x 720 pixels. To make video clips like this appear at full-screen, right-click on the clip in the Editor pane and choose Transform ⇨ Fit to Frame from the menu that appears. (The After image here shows you the results.) Your video may not look as sharp as true 1080 HD video, but it will be less distracting than having your video change size.

ADDING A VOICEOVER TO YOUR GAMEPLAY VIDEO

When putting together a video of your gameplay, you may want to add in a *voiceover* — an audio commentary that goes deep into the moments of your video and analyzes why a specific strategy works or doesn't work. How do you put one of those together, exactly?

Voiceovers can be easy to work into a video project. Though HitFilm Express doesn't offer a built-in voiceover option, incorporating a voiceover isn't hard. First, download Audacity (http://www.audacityteam.org) to install audio recording software for your voiceover.

TIP

Yes, you could use OBS to create a voiceover, but Audacity is designed to make audio editing simple and easy. And, like HitFilm Express and OBS, Audacity is free and safe to download.

SPEAKING WITH AUTHORITY

If you decide to add a voiceover, you need to do some things before recording your accompanying commentary:

» **Know what you're going to say.** Making up your commentary as you record isn't easy. In fact it is really, *really* hard. Once you have arranged all your gameplay footage on your timeline, watch it again and again, to make notes about what you're going to say and at what point. Then write your script if you think you need one.

» **Speak with confidence.** When recording your voice for your video, you need to be confident in what you're sharing. Think about your favorite teachers. One reason they're good at teaching is that they speak with authority and confidence.

REMEMBER

This is your YouTube video, and this is your breakdown of gameplay. Stand by your words.

» **Edit out any mistakes.** No recording is perfect on the first try. You *will* make mistakes. If you do, find a good place to stop, and then try again. Make sure to edit out any mistakes.

» **Be ready to review.** Before exporting your video from HitFilm Express and uploading your video to YouTube, review it again. Maybe get someone else to review it too. You want it to be right before you make it public.

RECORDING AND EDITING A VOICEOVER FOR YOUR GAMEPLAY VIDEO

After you install Audacity and launch it on your computer, recording a voiceover is a breeze:

1 **In Audacity, set the audio input for your microphone.**

If you look in the top left of the Audacity screen, you can see a little Microphone icon next to the drop-down menu of detected audio input devices.

Your menu will depend on your PC setup. If you use a headset for gaming, Audacity should see it.

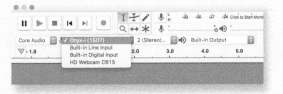

2 **Click the red Record button in Audacity's playback controls.**

Audacity creates a new track and begins recording. As you speak, you should see a *waveform* (an image of your voice, similar to the audio you see when working with video) being created.

3 **When you're done with your voiceover, click Stop in the playback controls.**

4 **Use the Rewind button to go back to the beginning of your audio recording and listen to your commentary.**

If everything sounds great, you're done! If you feel you need to edit something out — maybe you paused too long at one point, or your dog started barking —you have a few more steps to take.

5 **Find the segment that you want to edit.**

6 **Click the Selection tool and then click-and-drag across the unwanted segment.**

Segment to be cut

7 Press the Delete key (Mac) or the Backspace key (Windows) to remove the audio.

8 Review the clip. If the edit sounds "weird" to you, undo the edit by choosing Edit ⇨ Undo Delete from the main menu or by pressing Cmd+Z (Mac) or Ctrl+Z (Windows).

You're allowed multiple undo actions in Audacity, allowing you to go back to the beginning of your editing, just in case you aren't happy.

REMEMBER

9 When you're done editing your voiceover, choose File ⇨ Export ⇨ Export Audio from the main menu.

10 In the Export Audio dialog box that appears, name your file, choose a Save location, and choose an audio format from the File Type menu: AIF for a Mac computer or WAV for Windows.

11 Click the Save button to export your audio.

ADDING A VOICEOVER TO YOUR HITFILM PROJECT

Your voiceover is now ready to incorporate into your video project with these simple steps:

1 In HitFilm Express, go to the Media pane, click Import, navigate to wherever you saved your voiceover, select it, and then click Open.

2 Click-and-drag the audio clip from the Media pane to the Audio 2 track in the Editor pane.

3 Place the voiceover wherever you want it to begin.

4 Click the Toggle Track/Object Envelopes tool found just underneath the Audio 1 Track label, and then click-and-drag the white line in the middle of the Audio 1 track down to 40.00, in order to lower the gameplay's volume.

When you incorporate a voiceover, the audio of the commentary, not the gameplay itself, should be the focus. Lowering the audio level of the gameplay audio track means that your voiceover will be clearly heard.

EXPORTING YOUR HITFILM PROJECT FOR YOUTUBE

This is it. You've made a video for your YouTube channel. All that's left is for you to do is to get your video out of HitFilm Express and off to YouTube:

1 **When you think your video is ready, click the Export button in the upper right of the Editor pane, and then choose Contents from the menu that appears.**

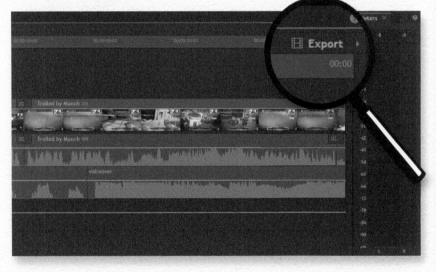

The Contents command looks at all video and audio in the Editor pane and exports it as a final file.

The Contents workspace should be divided into two screens:

» **Project:** The main window, where any open projects and their details appear

» **Queue:** The window that shows what projects or sections of projects are waiting to be exported

2 **In the Project window, you're asked to select your default preset resolution; choose YouTube 1080p HD.**

3 **You can leave the Output setting in the Queue window on the default location or click the location to change where you want the project exported.**

4 **Click the Start Exporting button at the bottom of the Queue window.**

The specifications of your computer, the chosen format, and the length of the project determine how long the processing of the video will take. In any event, you hear a chime when the export is finished.

5 **Locate the file on your computer and watch the video to make sure everything exported properly.**

6 **Follow the steps in the next project to upload your gameplay video to YouTube.**

SHOWING YOUR VIDEO TO YOUR FAMILY AND FRIENDS IS GREAT FUN. But you may want to share it with even more people. YouTube is the perfect place to do that. The website gets billions of views every day, and some of its videos have been viewed hundreds of millions of times.

In this project, we show you how to set up a YouTube channel and upload your video to YouTube. The steps that you take depend on whether you edited your video in iMovie or Filmora or another program.

GET A GOOGLE ACCOUNT

Before you can upload your video to YouTube, you need to create a Google account.

In most countries, you have to be age 13 or older to set up a Google account. Get permission from a parent or guardian before you start. They might even be able and willing to help.

These steps assume that you don't already have a Google account. If you already have one, go to www.youtube.com and skip to Step 6.

Follow these steps to create your Google account:

1 **Go to** www.google.com**.**

2 **Click Sign In.**

Sign In is in the top right of the Google home page.

If you're younger than 13, stop right there! Ask your parents to set up an account.

3 **Click the Create Account link.**

It's below the Sign In form. You're asked whether you want an account for yourself or for your business. Choose For Yourself.

4 **Fill in the Create Your Google Account form. Click Next as you complete each screen.**

You'll be asked for a few different pieces of information, like your name (it's OK to use your real name here), your email address, and a password. You're also asked for a phone number, which is optional, but it's a good idea to enter one. It's really helpful if you ever forget your password and need to access your account. If you don't have your own phone number, ask a parent or guardian if you can use theirs.

5 **Accept the privacy policy and terms of service by clicking I Agree (assuming, of course, that you do accept the terms).**

Congratulations! You now have a shiny new Google account.

TIP

The privacy policy and terms of service are quite long and complicated, and if you're not comfortable reading and understanding them, ask your parent or guardian to review and agree on your behalf.

6 **Visit www.youtube.com. You should be signed in already, but if you're not, click Sign In.**

The Sign In link is in the top right of the YouTube home page. Use the email address and password for the Google account you just created. You'll be signed in and land back on the YouTube home page.

7 **Click your Profile icon.**

The icon is in the top right of the YouTube home page.

TIP

By default, your Profile icon is just your initial. If you want to upload a photo as your Profile icon, you can click on Manage Your Google Account and update the icon under the Personal Info section.

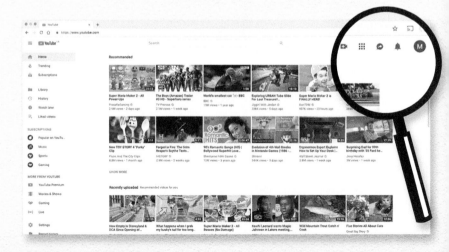

8 Choose <mark>Your Channel from the drop-down menu</mark> that appears.

You'll see the message Use YouTube As, where you get to set your name. Don't use your real name; instead, choose a channel name that's related to your style of videos. Sometimes, the most random and crazy channel names are the most popular. When you've decided, click Create Channel. Boom! Your channel has been born and is ready for your video uploads.

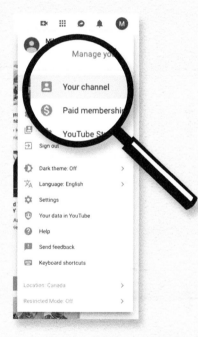

TIP

When you're in your channel, click the Customize Channel button and get creative. It's a great idea to make your channel uniquely yours by tweaking some of its settings. You can change your channel art (the big banner image across the top of your channel), add featured channels, which can be some of the channels you like, and on the About tab you can edit your channel description and add links to your other sites.

Don't share any personal information, like your contact details, when you're customizing your channel settings. For example, popular YouTubers sometimes list on the About tab a contact email address for their business manager. If you get superfamous, you can use contact information for a parent or guardian or even your manager, agent, or business representative, for all those brands that want to work with you.

UPLOAD A VIDEO TO YOUTUBE

These steps are for you if you *didn't* use iMovie or Filmora to edit your video:

1 Go to www.youtube.com **and log in to your YouTube account.**

2 **Click the little Camera icon in the upper right.**

3 **Choose Upload Video from the menu that appears.**

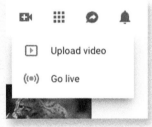

You have the option to go live. YouTube's policy is that if you're under 13 years old, you can broadcast live only if you have an adult present. If you do broadcast live, be sure not to reveal any personal information, like your name, contact information, or location.

4 **Click Select Files to Upload and find your video file.**

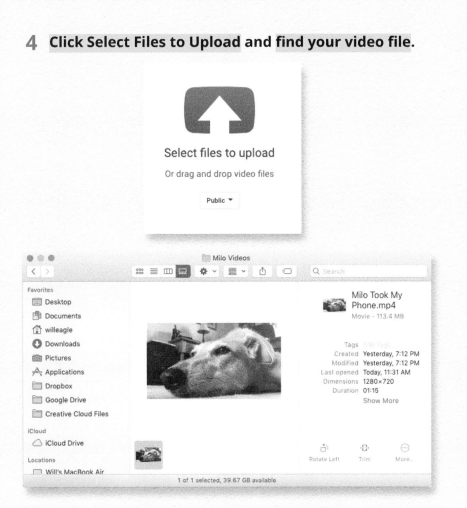

TIP

Have your parent or guardian check your videos before you upload them. Not only can they make sure you're being smart and safe, they might have some fun tips on how to make your videos better.

5 Click Open.

Your video starts uploading immediately. A progress bar shows the upload process.

6 Wait until your video is done being processed and then enter your video's title and description in the spaces YouTube provides.

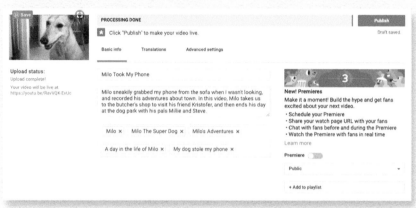

7 Choose a thumbnail image from the three you see below the Tags box.

TIP

For more on writing great titles and choosing the best thumbnails, take a look at the section "Titles, Thumbnails, and Testing," later in this project.

8 Click Publish in the top right of the page.

Your video is on YouTube! You'll get a link so that you can share the video with your family and friends.

TIP

At any time, you can access your YouTube Studio to see all the videos you've uploaded, change advanced settings for each video (like turning off comments), see how many people have watched your videos in the Analytics section, plus a whole lot more. To do this, click your profile image and choose Your Channel in the upper right, and then click on YouTube Studio. For more on everything you can do, see the "Your YouTube Studio" section, later in this project.

WARNING

When you're uploading your videos, YouTube uses its sophisticated tools to determine whether your content uses anyone else's copyrighted work. Having the copyright to something means owning the right to use it without needing anyone's permission. For example, Beyoncé (and her team) own the copyright to her songs, videos, logos, and anything they have created — because they created it! You have the copyright to any content you create. If you use video clips from your favorite movie or if you use the music of your favorite musician, YouTube might block your video from being displayed because YouTube knows that you don't own the copyright to that content — it belongs to Beyoncé. You're only allowed to upload videos you have created yourself, so don't upload anything you don't own. YouTube will apply a strike to your account and can ban you if you do it too many times.

SHARE YOUR VIDEO TO YOUTUBE WITH IMOVIE

Follow these steps if you edited your video in iMovie and want to upload the video to YouTube:

1 Make sure you have a YouTube account.

REMEMBER

Hey, you! Yes, you. You have to be at least 13 years old to have a YouTube account. Ask your parents for permission to use one of their accounts, or ask for help setting up one. Setting up an account, that is — not setting up your parents.

2 Open your video in iMovie.

 3 Click the Share icon on the top toolbar.

You get a list of sharing options.

4 Click the YouTube logo.

You see the settings for your video.

5 Click in the title box and type a new title, if you want to.

Your title should be a short but clear description of the main theme of your video.

TIP

For more on writing great titles, take a look at the section "Titles, Thumbnails, and Testing," later in this project.

6 Add a description about the film by clicking in the Description box.

A great description tells what your video is about, says who is in it, links to topics you talk about, and links to your social media sites so that your fans can follow you outside of YouTube.

7 Add tag words, if you want to.

If you do, add a comma between the words or phrases.

WARNING

Although iMovie lets you choose the size of your video, it's best to leave it at the default (automatic) setting.

8 Choose something from the Category menu.

9 From the Privacy menu, choose Public.

WARNING

You can leave the Privacy option set to Private if you only want people you know to see your film. Just keep in mind that anything you put online isn't very private. If you want your video to be found by anyone, change your privacy settings to Public. Check with your parents first before setting your video to Public.

10 Click the Sign In button on the left to connect iMovie to your YouTube account.

A new Sign In dialog box specifically for YouTube appears.

11 **Click the Sign In button** in this new dialog box.

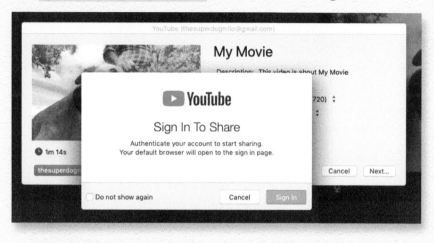

If this is the first time you're signing in to your YouTube account from iMovie, a browser opens and you're asked to give iMovie permission to access your YouTube account. Read the terms and click Allow. If you're already signed in, you'll see your YouTube account email address in place of the Sign In button.

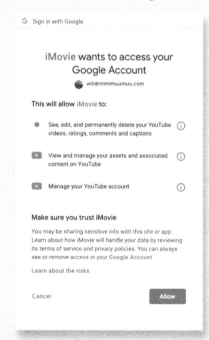

12 **Return to iMovie and click Next.**

13 **Read the YouTube terms of service. If you agree, click Publish.**

Your video is uploaded to your account on YouTube. When it's done, you see a message in the top right of the screen.

To change your title and tags, who can comment on your video, and other settings, jump to the "Your YouTube Studio" section, later in this project. (*Tags* are words that people use for searching. If you come up with the right tags for your video, there's a better chance that folks will find it when searching.)

SHARE YOUR VIDEO TO YOUTUBE WITH FILMORA

Follow these steps if you edited your video in Filmora and want to upload the video to YouTube:

1 **Make sure you have a YouTube account.**

REMEMBER

You probably know the score by now: If you're younger than 13 years, ask your parents for permission to use their accounts. You might have to ask your parents to set up an account.

2 Open your video project in Filmora.

3 Click Export on the top toolbar and choose Upload to YouTube from the menu that appears.

If you have the free version, you're prompted to either continue with the free version or purchase a plan. *Remember:* The free version shows a Filmora watermark on your final video. Once you continue, you' then see the settings for your video.

4 Click in the title box and type a new title, if you want to.

Your title should be a short but clear description of the main theme of your video.

TIP

For more on writing great titles, take a look at the section "Titles, Thumbnails, and Testing," later in this project.

5 Add a description about the film by clicking in the Description box.

A great description tells what your video is about, says who is in it, links to things you talk about, and links to your social media sites so that your fans can follow you outside of YouTube.

6 Add tag words, if you want to.

If you do, add a comma between the words or phrases.

 WARNING

Although you have the option of changing your video settings here, it's best to leave them at the default (automatic) settings.

7 **From the Privacy menu, choose Public.**

 WARNING

You can leave Privacy set to Private if you want only people you know to see your film. Just keep in mind that anything you put online isn't very private. If you want your video to be found by anyone, change your privacy settings to Public. Check with your parents first before setting your video to Public.

8 **Click the Sign In button under the YouTube logo.**

9 **Sign in to your account.**

If this is the first time you're signing in to your YouTube account from Filmora, a browser opens and you're asked to give Filmora permission to access your YouTube account. Read the terms and click Allow.

YouTube Authorization ×

Wondershare Filmora wants to
access your Google Account

nick@filmmakingforkids.com

This will allow Wondershare Filmora to:

▶ Manage your YouTube videos ⓘ

▶ View your YouTube account ⓘ

Make sure that you trust Wondershare Filmora

You may be sharing sensitive info with this site or app. Find
out how Wondershare Filmora will handle your data by
reviewing its terms of service and privacy policies. You can
always see or remove access in your Google Account.

Find out about the risks

Cancel **Allow**

10 When you're ready, click Export.

A new dialog box appears, showing the progress of
your video upload to YouTube.

When your upload is complete, the dialog box will
display the YouTube video link and give you the option
to locate the video file on your computer by clicking
the Find Target button.

×

Step: Upload completed.

Total: 100%

URL: https://www.youtube.com/watch?v=BX4sBGjM3P4

When Done: Sound reminder ⌄ | Find Target | Remove Mark

REMEMBER

If you are using the free version of Filmora, you can remove the watermark by clicking on the Remove Mask button to buy the full version of the software.

To change your title and tags, who can comment on your video, and other settings, jump to the "Your YouTube Studio" section, later in this project.

TITLES, THUMBNAILS, AND TESTING

The difference between a YouTube channel with great videos and a YouTube channel with great videos and lots of video views is simple: It's all about titles, thumbnails, and testing. Nailing your title and thumbnail and testing what works best makes all the difference in attracting lots of views and fans.

TITLES

The title is one of the most important strategies to get people to choose to watch your video. A great title is a clear description of what your video is all about, because people like to know what they're going to get. You can try a few different creative approaches to crafting your title:

» **The question:** You can write a title that uses a question; for example, "Can I eat 100 chicken nuggets?" This style is especially good for challenge videos and for encouraging people to click to find out if you could do it! (By the way, the answer for us is yes. We have no regrets.)

» **The statement:** Simply make a statement about the video, such as "How I retouch my Instagram photos." It's clear and tells people exactly what your video is about.

» **The clickbait:** We would bet that you've clicked on a similar-sounding video from a famous YouTuber: "I am quitting this channel forever. **NOT CLICKBAIT **" only to find that they weren't telling the truth. *Clickbait* is information designed to be clicked, by enticing people with shocking or surprising headlines that often turn out to be untrue.

» **Try your own:** Get creative with your titles, and find what works for you. As long as it's a compelling and accurate reflection of your video, you're good to go.

THUMBNAILS

Take a look at your favorite YouTubers to see how they make their thumbnails. You'll notice that the thumbnails are eye-catching and encourage you to click them. When you upload your video to YouTube, three still frames from your video are automatically picked for you to choose from. If your account is *verified* (that is, you've confirmed that you are you!), and if it's in *good standing* (you haven't broken any rules), you may be eligible for a special feature that lets you add your own, custom thumbnail that you can create separately from your video.

Follow these steps to set up custom thumbnails:

1 **Log in to your YouTube account.**

2 **Click your Profile icon and choose Your Channel from the menu that appears.**

   Your Profile icon is in the top right of the YouTube page.

3 **Click YouTube Studio.**

4 **Click in the Video section on the menu on the left side.**

5 **Choose a video to edit by clicking its title.**

Again, if you've already *verified* your account (proven that it's you), and it's in good standing (you haven't broken any YouTube policies), you have the option, just beneath the Description box, to upload a custom thumbnail you've saved to your computer. If you haven't verified your account, clicking on the Custom Thumbnail box gives you a link to get verified. YouTube uses an automated call or text message to send you a verification code.

6 **Click the Custom Thumbnail box, navigate to where you saved your custom thumbnail, select it, and then click Open.**

Your custom thumbnail is uploaded to YouTube.

Your custom thumbnail image should be as large as possible. It should

» Have a resolution of 1280 x 720 (with a minimum width of 640 pixels)

» Be uploaded in image formats such as JPG, GIF, BMP, or PNG

» Remain under the 2MB limit

» Use a 16:9 aspect ratio, if possible, because it's the most commonly used ratio in YouTube players and previews

Follow these other tips to make the best thumbnails possible:

» Make sure your thumbnail clearly shows what your video is all about — don't mislead people.

» People's faces tend to perform better than anything else, so include yourself!

» Make use of bright colors to attract attention.

» You can use text to provide extra information about your video, but keep it to a word or two.

TESTING

Testing means experimenting with your titles and thumbnails to see what works best, and taking a planned approach will help you figure out the secret recipe quicker. Let's say you're making a video showing you baking a cake. You could make two videos (and two cakes!) and title one "How to make a bunny rabbit cake" and title the other "The Cutest Bunny Cake That Ever Hopped Off The Table." You could choose a thumbnail showing you holding the cake in the first video and then feature just the cake in the second video's thumbnail. Upload both and see which one performs better. You might find that more fun and creative titles (like the bunny hopping off the table) and that thumbnails featuring you (versus just the cake) work best. That'll help you make the best choices when you make more videos, so experiment, try different things, and see which titles and thumbnails attract the most views.

YOUR YOUTUBE STUDIO

There's so much to explore after you've uploaded your video, and you'll find a ton of features and tools in your new YouTube Studio. It's the back-end tool you can use to control your channel and videos and to tweak lots of settings.

To get into YouTube Studio, follow these steps:

1 Log in to your YouTube account.

2 Click your Profile icon and choose Your Channel from the menu that appears.

Your Profile icon is in the top right of the YouTube page.

3 Click YouTube Studio.

Your YouTube Studio appears onscreen.

THE DASHBOARD

When you first log in to your YouTube Studio, you land on your Dashboard. This is a great place to start when you want to see a snapshot of how your videos and channel are doing, along with tips, tricks, and resources from the YouTube team to help you make your videos even better.

Here's what's on your dashboard:

» **Videos:** You see videos you've recently uploaded along with how many video views they have, how long people watched, and their total amount of watch time — that's all the minutes people watched added together. (See the later sidebar "Watch your watch time" for more on watch time.)

» **News:** There's a section for news, which features videos and updates directly from the folks at YouTube. They give you tips and tricks on how to do Everything YouTube, along with news about changes they might make. Watch these videos because they're a great way to learn more about YouTube and how it all works. You also get expert advice from YouTube creators as well as custom ideas, just for you, to help you grow your audience.

» **Analytics:** A snapshot of your *analytics* — that's the numbers of views, subscribers, and more — are also on your dashboard. It tells you information like how many total subscribers you have and how many video views you've had in the last 28 days.

VIDEOS

The Videos section is where all your videos live. You can choose a video and edit any of its information — its title and description, for example — and tweak advanced settings. Just make sure you click Save in the upper right so that your changes are saved.

Try changing some of the following video settings:

» **Edit the title.** If you made a spelling mistake, for example, this is your chance to correct it.

» **Edit your description.** Make sure to include details about what your video features and any relevant links you think your fans will want to check out.

» **Tweak your thumbnail.** You can change the thumbnail that appears whenever someone searches for your video.

» **Change the privacy settings.** If you decide that you don't want your video to be on YouTube any more, you can change its visibility from Public, where anyone can find and watch it, to Private, so that no one can find it unless you give them the link. You can even set it to Unlisted, which means that no one can see it except you.

» **Add more tags.** Twenty or so is a good number.

You'll notice a tab labeled Advanced. Most people don't need to change many of these settings, but take a look. You might like to change the category that applies to your video. Nick has listed Milo's video under Pets & Animals.

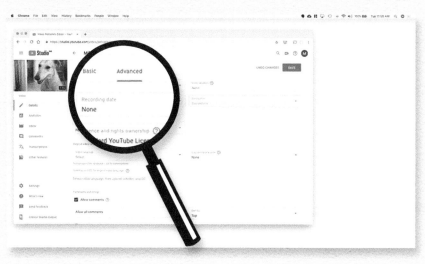

ANALYTICS

Analytics refers to all the data and reports that YouTube gives you so that you can see how your videos and channel are doing. It really just means all the numbers you might be interested in! The team at YouTube has built in some powerful tools so that you can see just how much your efforts are paying off. It's a great idea to spend some time here because it can help you learn what works so that you can make more content that people want to watch.

Browse around the Analytics section to see how many people have viewed your videos, which videos are your best performers, and even info like how long people watch. Don't get disheartened if you don't have millions of views in the first few weeks of uploading. It can take time to perfect your videos and build an audience. Keep at it, and the views will come!

Take a look at these reports:

» **The Overview:** This is a great place to start, especially if you're new to looking at data and reports. You can see how many times people have viewed your videos all added up together, how long they watched (see the later sidebar "Watch your watch time"), how many subscribers you've added, and which videos are your top performers. The drop-down menu in the upper right lets you change dates so that you can see how things are going over the last week, month, or year or since you first published a video.

» **Reach Viewers:** This report is all about understanding how appealing your video is to your audience. You should look at these three important labeled numbers:

» *Impressions* tells you how many times your videos were recommended to people; that's all the times YouTube showed your title and thumbnail to someone — perhaps when people were searching.

» *Impressions Click-Through-Rate* tells you whether you caught viewers' attention and got them to click and watch. Click-through-rate simply means "Of all the times we showed your title and thumbnails, this percentage of people clicked to watch." If your title and thumbnail were shown 2,000 times (2,000 *impressions*) and you got 87 people clicking and watching, you got a click through rate of 4.35 percent. (That's pretty good, by the way.) The higher your click-through rate, the more attention people are paying to your title and thumbnail.

» *Views* is just what you're thinking: It's how many total video views you've had. The number labeled Unique Viewers is how many individual people watched. You'll likely have more views than unique viewers because some people like to watch more than one of your videos or watch them more than once.

In this report, you also learn how people found your video. Take a look at the box labeled Traffic Sources Type — it tells you whether people found your videos because of a search, a suggested video recommendation after watching another video, or a playlist.

WATCH YOUR WATCH

OK, so watch time gets mentioned a lot, but *what is it?* Before we answer, we have to dispel a common myth about YouTube. A lot of people think that the best videos are the ones that have the most views, but we think you should try this little trick: Go to YouTube and search for a video (any video), and look at the results you see. We would bet that the videos listed from top to bottom aren't in order of the most number of views. So why would a video with 40,000 views get listed above a video with 1.2 million views? Well, the answer is *watch time* — YouTube wants to keep people watching, so it rewards videos that have more watch time, not more views, by recommending them more. For example, you might make a video teaching how to perform a magic trick you've perfected. If someone watches it and then watches another hour of videos all about magic tricks (yours or anyone else's), that racks up a lot of watch time. If, on the other hand, the person watched your video and then decided to take their dog for a walk when it ended, your video didn't add up to a lot of watch time. Simply put: If your video encourages people to watch more YouTube, it gets recommended before other videos do — even videos with more views. And that's why it's so important to watch your watch time: The more watch time you have, the better!

» **Interest Viewers:** If the Reach Viewers report is all about how you found an audience, the Interest Viewers report tells you what your audience enjoyed most about your videos. You see a number for watch time, which is the number of minutes people have watched your videos (take a look at the nearby sidebar "Watch your watch time") and a number for the average view duration, which is the average amount of time they watched. You can also find a list of your top videos in this report. Take a look and see which videos do the best. (Can you come up with ideas on how to make more videos like your best performers?)

» **Build an Audience:** This report is really interesting. YouTube reaches billions of people all over the world, and this report tells you all about them. You can learn about their age and gender and which country they're watching from. If you're getting a lot of views from another country, maybe you can come up with some videos that would appeal primarily to them.

COMMENTS

The Comments section shows you a collection of all comments across all your video uploads. It's an easy place to respond to your fans, even if it's just your well-meaning grandmother. Learn more about comments by taking a look at the later sidebar, "Comments . . . in moderation." If you want to turn off comments, you can turn them off for specific videos or for all videos.

For specific videos, follow these steps:

1 In YouTube Studio, click on Videos.

2 Click on the video whose comments you want to turn off.

3 **Click Advanced and uncheck the Allow Comments box.**

4 **Click Save.**

To turn off comments from all videos, follow these steps:

1 **In YouTube Studio, click Settings.**

2 **Choose Upload Defaults from the navigation menu on the left.**

3 **Go to the Advanced tab and click the Disable Comments radio button.**

4 **Click Save.**

All comments are now disabled on all videos.

Settings

General   Essentials   Extras   Advanced

Channel

Upload defaults   Video language   Caption certification ⑦
                           Select   ▾   None   ▾

Community

Other settings   Community contributions
                           Off   ▾

                           Comm

                           ○ Hold po
                             for review   riate comments

                           ○ Hold all comm
                                                     w

                           ◉ Disable comme

                           ☑ Users can   or this vi

                                              CANCEL   SAVE

TIP

Lots more features are available in YouTube Studio, with more being added all the time, so go explore!

COMMENTS . . . IN MODERATION

One of the greatest things about YouTube is that when you post videos, you'll get comments from people who watch. They'll tell you what they like, and they'll also tell you what they don't like. That's OK because it can help you make your videos better, but sometimes people can be mean-spirited — so the trick with comments is to never take things personally. Instead, focus on the nice things people have to say and the comments that help you improve — and ignore the haters. You can change your comment settings so that you get to approve them before they appear on your videos, or you can turn comments off entirely.

HOW TO MAKE GREAT VIDEOS

Making great videos that people like to watch is as simple as ABCD. Check out these guidelines to make awesome videos.

A IS FOR ATTRACT THEIR ATTENTION

After clicking on your video, people quickly decide, in the first few seconds, whether they want to watch it.

So it's vital to attract their attention and hook them in immediately. There are a few tricks to do this:

» **Use your YouTube voice.** No, really, it's a thing. Watch your favorite YouTubers, and you'll see that they all follow a similar pattern of speech. It's a sing-song, upbeat, and energetic way of speaking. Before you hit Record, get yourself revved up and ready to go!

» **Use quick cuts.** A popular technique to keep someone's attention is to use *quick cuts,* which means cutting out the "dead air" in whatever you're talking about. It brings a pace and an energy that keeps people watching.

» **Be visual.** YouTube is all about being visual, so get creative with your visuals. Show people, don't tell. Take them on the adventure with you. Give them the behind-the-scenes view. People want to see, not to be told.

» **Pets are golden.** It won't surprise you to learn that pets work well in videos. Go ask your cat nicely (he might say yes) or involve the dog (she's happy to help) in your videos, because people love to see animals. You should pay them fairly in treats for their work.

B IS FOR BE YOURSELF

Almost every YouTuber will agree that being yourself is vitally important. If you aren't authentically you, your viewers and fans won't like it. So, from the start of your video all the way to the end, make sure to be yourself. That "brand" of you is what people like most. For example, think about your look: You can create your own, special style that you always wear so that people know it's you. Maybe it's the way you do your hair, or as simple as the T-shirt you wear. Or maybe it's the jokes or catchphrases you always use that make you recognizable and uniquely you. People want to see the person they know and love, so emphasize what makes you *you*. That's what separates you from everyone else on YouTube.

C IS FOR CONNECTION

If your video is long — say, 25 minutes or more — you *have* to maintain a connection with your audience so that they stick around and watch until the end. Usually, that's all about telling a great story, because, if you aren't bored, you aren't boring! Keep the energy going and cut out any boring or low-energy moments. Some of the best YouTubers make videos of themselves talking to the camera for ages, and people love it! They tell great stories, they make you laugh, they keep it interesting — that's a real talent. It's easy to make a video where you *think* you're being interesting but you're actually making people yawn — so watch the footage you made and cut out anything that feels dull. It's better to have a shorter-but-more-fun video than a longer video that people might abandon halfway through.

D IS FOR DIRECT THEM ON WHAT TO DO NEXT

A great video always ends by telling the viewer what to do next. Try out some of the following suggestions:

» Encourage them to watch another video.

» Ask them to check out a website.

» Tell them to take an action, like go outside and find adventure.

» Always, always, *always* ask them to like, comment, and subscribe.

WAYS TO ATTRACT MORE VIEWS!

Have you ever wondered how some videos get so many views? You can try lots of tricks for increasing your video's number of *views* — or how many people watch it.

Here are several tricks to help you draw more views:

» **Hook them with your title and thumbnail.** Here's the deal: Your title and thumbnail are the most important info to get right for all your videos. When you're browsing YouTube for something to watch, it's the title-and-thumbnail combo that attracts your attention and encourages you to click, so it's crucial to crack. Check out the section "Titles, Thumbnails, and Testing," earlier in this project.

» **Add a great description.** Lots of people don't include a description, but a good one can make a difference. Your description should explain what the audience will see when watching your video. The description can include details on what you talk about, who's in the video, any links you reference, and any other relevant details. You don't need to spend ages writing a long description, but adding more doesn't hurt anything, because it gives YouTube more clues to what your video is all about. This is a chance to sell your video, so go for it.

» **Use the best tags.** *Tags* are words that people use for searching. Using smart tags increases the chance that people will find your video. Use words from your title and description, plus any words that are related to what happens in your video. *Tag words* are related to your video — they help people search for it. When you're thinking about what tags to use, think about how people might find your video. How would you look for your own video? What search words would you enter? What words are related to the video? Is it a *funny video*, a *documentary*, or a *short film?* Does it show a *cat jumping* or *dog snoring?* Or a *place* or *landmark*? Don't use unrelated words. That could confuse people and make you lose viewers.

» **Involve your audience.** Ask your audience what they like about your videos and what they want to see next. The audience is a great source of inspiration for new video ideas. Over time, you'll get better and better at making videos that people truly enjoy watching. Check out some of your favorite YouTubers to see what they're making, and see if you can bring your own, unique spin to the same idea.

» **Make it shareable, and tell everyone.** Be proud of your video! Tell people about it. Email and share your YouTube video link with your friends and family and ask them to share it too. In the video itself, make sure you ask people to like and share it. (If you don't ask, you don't get!) You can post comments on videos that are similar to yours. Ask people to watch your video and to like and share. This is also a great way to get people to subscribe to your channel. Just don't spam people.

TIP

Spam isn't just a delicious canned meat product! It's the name on the Internet for when you bombard people, especially people you don't know, with loads of irrelevant messages. It's a great way to get blocked, banned, and lose friends, everywhere on the web. Eat spam, but don't spam.

» **Make it consistent.** Most popular YouTubers consistently upload videos, — at least once a week — and their videos tend to have the same look, feel, tone, and content. Find the topic that you're passionate about and that you want to make lots of videos about, and then map out a plan to make a video every week or every few weeks. The more consistent you are with the videos you make and how often you upload, the more likely you'll draw lots of fans.

» **Keep it real.** You can create a character (look at Miranda Sings, who has 10 million subscribers), or you can be yourself, but whichever route you choose, make sure you stay true to yourself. The best YouTubers are really popular because they're uniquely themselves and they never pretend to be someone or something else. People will love your videos for you, so keep it real, stay authentic, and be you.

» **Always ask people to subscribe.** Every YouTuber's video should end by asking people to subscribe! Ask people to like, to comment, and to subscribe to your YouTube channel. Consider subscribing to other YouTube users. Sometimes, if you subscribe to other people's channels, they return the favor. If they don't, ask them to. Attracting more subscribers is the best way to draw more views.

» **Create playlists.** A *playlist* is a bunch of videos that play, one after the other. A playlist can have videos that are related by subject (like, oh, we don't know, *dogs*) from you and other YouTubers. If your video is about your dog, think about making a playlist with all the funniest dog videos you can find and then include yours.

» **Add a good channel image.** Add an image to your channel that grabs the people who are browsing YouTube. Choose an image that goes with the videos in your channel. It might be a screen shot from one of your films or a picture of the cat that stars in your video.

GLOSSARY

AS YOU READ THROUGH THIS BOOK, SOME WORDS WILL BE NEW TO YOU. If you're not sure about a word I've used in this book, you can refer to this list.

action   A term called by the director during the filming of a scene to let cast and crew know that a take has started.

angle   The position of the camera with respect to the subject.

audio   The sound that is recorded when filming.

blockbuster   A large-scale (really, really big) film with a high production budget (lots of money to spend making it) and usually released globally into theaters.

boom   A long pole with a microphone attached. Booms are usually held above the actors to record sound in a scene.

camcorder   A video camera, which is a device used to record footage.

camera phone   A cellphone device that can capture still images and record video footage.

cast   The group of actors who are in a film or video.

character   A person in a story, usually fictional.

clapperboard   A board where you write the details of the film shoot. You hold it in front of the camera to introduce a scene during filming. Traditionally chalk was used to write the details, but now marker pens are used. A clapperboard is sometimes referred to as a slate.

crew   A group of people behind the scenes or behind the camera who are involved in the making of a film or video.

cut   A term called by the director during filming to let the cast and crew know that a take is over.

development   The process of building and creating a film.

dialogue   The words spoken by the characters in a film or video.

director   The person who tells the actors and crew what to do. The director also chooses camera angles and what shots to use in the video.

distribution   The steps you need to take in order to get your video in front of an audience.

editing   The process of putting the film footage and clips together after filming.

editing tool   The software on a computer used to edit video.

effect   A visual or audio technique used to enhance or change the look or sound of a video clip. You can add effects during filming or editing.

establishing shot   This is the first shot to appear in a new scene, so it sets up, or establishes, the scene.

filmmaker   The person who creates a film or movie.

fictional   Based on a story that is imagined by the writer and not normally based on fact.

FireWire cable   A way of transferring data and video footage from a camera to a computer. FireWire connections can also be referred to as IEEE 1394.

focus   The sharpness of an image.

frame   A single image taken from the many images captured within footage. Also known as a still.

HD   High definition (for a crisper picture).

import   Saving video footage to a computer from a camera, tape, or media card.

lens   A device attached to the camera that uses glass to focus on a subject.

lighting   To provide light to a scene. Also, lighting includes the devices (like a lamp) that provide light to a scene.

lines   Dialogue (words) in the script performed by the actors.

location   A place or area used to film a scene.

media card   A small storage device that stores the audio or video being recorded by the camera. CompactFlash (CF), Secure Digital (SD), MicroSD, MiniSD, and SxS cards are some of the media cards for video cameras.

microphone   A device used to record sound when filming. Also called a mic.

model release form   A signed record stating that someone has given you permission to film them for a video.

monitor   A mini screen that lets you see what the camera captures as it films and review what you have recorded.

nonfictional   A film or video using facts or real events starring the actual people involved in the events.

pre-production   Getting all the prep work done so your filming can go smoothly.

production   The things you do when you're actually making your video — rehearsing your actors, setting the scene, and doing the actual filming.

post-production   The work you put into a movie after filming.

prop   Any item used by an actor.

reel   A length of filmstrip wrapped around a metal wheel for viewing on a projector. Film was used to record movies before the age of digital video (and is still used sometimes). Even digital movies are often sent to theaters on film reels. An average movie requires three to five reels of film.

scene   A series of shots filmed at one location to tell a section of the story.

schedule   A plan of the day's filming that shows the times and details of shots to be filmed.

script   A document with details of a story to film, including the scenes and dialogue.

set   An area built where a scene can be filmed.

shoot   To film, or record, video footage.

shot   One section of footage recorded by the camera from start to finish.

shot list   A list used by the crew showing the shots to be filmed within a scene.

sound effects   Sounds added to a film when editing.

storyboard   A series, or a bunch, of images created before filming. It helps you plan the shots to film.

subject   The person or object being filmed.

take One recorded performance of a scene during filming. Expect to shoot tens or hundreds of takes per scene (depending on how long the scene is).

tripod A support — usually 3-legged — you can use to keep your camera steady

upload Sending and saving a video from a computer to a website or server.

USB cable A cord you can attach to transfer footage from a camera to a computer.

voiceover A recorded voice used in a film or documentary. The speaker is not shown.

white balance A feature found in many digital cameras that lets you produce more natural colors by countering the distorting effects of some lighting sources

zoom Magnifying an object or subject when filming. Makes the subject appear closer or farther away.

ABOUT THE AUTHORS

Nick Willoughby is a UK-based filmmaker, director, actor, and writer who has a real enthusiasm and love for film. Nick's passion for filmmaking started when he wrote his first short film at the age of 18. Since then, he's been inspiring young people to bring their stories to life through the art of film.

Nick started his career as an actor and went on to experience a wide range of roles within the media industry, from camera operator to director. After offering his skills to schools as a film tutor and consultant, he set up Filmmaking for Kids, which aims to encourage and inspire young people to develop their creativity through the art of film. Nick now facilitates the courses at Filmmaking for Kids while writing and directing films, corporate videos, and commercials with his UK production company, 7 Stream Media.

Tee Morris is co-author of *Podcasting For Dummies, 3rd Edition* and *Twitch For Dummies*.

Will Eagle is author of *YouTube Marketing For Dummies*.

AUTHOR'S ACKNOWLEDGMENTS

Nick Willoughby

To be asked to write another book, *Making YouTube Videos*, was an honor and a surprise. It's only fair I acknowledge those who helped me along the way.

You wouldn't have this book in your hand if it weren't for the inspiration of executive editor Steve Hayes and the support from the fantastic Tonya Cupp and Paul Levesque.

A big thank you to the handsome Toby, for appearing in project opener images. Thank you also to Poppy, for being the camera operator, and to Ashish, Josh, and Paige, who appear in some of the figures throughout the book.

I also want to thank my dog, Milo, for agreeing to star in the YouTube video that accompanies this book. He is just the cutest dog ever and gives the best hugs — not so keen on the sloppy kisses, though.

I am especially grateful to my parents, for making me who I am. Without their love, support, patience, and constructive criticism, I would not be where I am today.

Lastly, I want to thank God for giving me my creative brain and for being my strength and inspiration.

PUBLISHER'S ACKNOWLEDGMENTS

Executive Editor:
Steven Hayes

Development Editors:
Tonya Maddox Cupp
and Paul Levesque

Copy Editor:
Becky Whitney

Production Editor:
Mohammed Zafar Ali

Special Help:
Christine Corry and
Fritz Wilbur Henderson

Sr. Editorial Assistant:
Cherie Case

Project Layout:
Galen Gruman

Creative Director:
Paul Dinovo

Marketing:
Melisa Duffy,
Lauren Noens,
Raichelle Weller

Launch Consultants:
John Helmus, John Scott